I Called Her Mary

A Memoir

by

Margaret M. O'Hagan
&
Thomas A. Gorman, Ed.D.

ISBN 978-0-578-98193-2

To *my* Mickey - the love of *my* life.

May God grant you always…

A sunbeam to warm you,
A moonbeam to charm you,
A sheltering Angel so nothing can harm you.
Laughter to cheer you.
Faithful friends near you.
And whenever you pray, Heaven to hear you.

Irish Blessing

And now these three remain: faith, hope and love.
But the greatest of these is love.

1 Corinthians 13:1

Foreword

Decisions are made every day. Decisions that range from what to wear to what path to follow in life. From the most simple to the most complex. Each decision slightly alters who we are, how we feel, and where we will go. We may make wrong decisions, but hopefully we learn from these mistakes. That is life. We pray to have the opportunity to live and learn from our decisions, make a better choice when the next opportunity arises, and see the results of our choices. However, life can throw some serious curveballs at us and we must be ready to swing. Sometimes, we get a little piece of that curveball and get to stay at the plate. Other times, we get the whole ball and nail it out of the park. Yet there are still times when we swing, miss, and feel like we will never have another chance at bat.

I can only imagine how absolutely alone my mother felt when she found out she was pregnant as a teenager in a conservative village in 1950s Ireland knowing her life would never be the same again. She was sent away in shame only to find courage and wisdom deep within her soul that led her to the greatest life, husband, and family; a family that would love her endlessly and respect her with a profound dignity that thrives today.

Being the only girl in the family until 2008 was a gift, but I longed to share with a sister. I was raised with encouragement, pride, and unselfish love. I couldn't wait to share my mom with the world because I believe the more people who meet and know the soul of my mother, the better off we all will be.

My mother taught me to be the woman I am today. To never settle! To be my best in all that I am and all that I do. As I age and see the depth of my mother's words and actions, she continues to amaze me with her strength.

So many times she could have been a victim, thrown her hands up, and said "I'm out." However, she never chose to quit – she kept swinging and never struck out. I am a proud Irish woman, raised by a proud Irish mother, and now I am raising proud Irish daughters. My mother is everything I hope to be and even though I know I will come up short, I will never stop swinging.

Margaret E. O'Hagan-Gorman
2019

Preface

Christmas Eve 2015, the noisiest of all the holidays, took place, as it always has, in the small basement of the O'Hagan household that is now only used once a year. Any guest will find an artificial Christmas tree with decorations up year-round proudly standing in the corner. Peg likes it that way. The stockings are nailed to the wall with each family member's name, including their dogs. These do not come down either.

Peg and I sat side by side cramped on her small basement couch. We were surrounded by thirty or so people, family and friends, who came to celebrate. The dimly lit room was filled with a cacophony of sounds stemming from children of all ages, an underscoring of Christmas songs spilling out from the 1970s stereo in the corner, and sometimes interrupted by a sports controversy bursting from the men over at the basement bar. The catered food was served on plastic plates, and the casual conversations were punctuated by random bursts of yelling and excitement. Amidst the noise, a silence overcame the room and I thought it was about time, so I did it. I was nervous to bring the topic up again; nervous she might get upset but also nervous she might say no. I took a sip of my drink and then asked Peg for the third and final time, "So...would you like me to write your life story?"

I was rejected twice before over the past seven years. This time she said, "I lived the story, Tom, and have spent a lifetime trying to forget it."

I had to push for this one last time. Peg's story is one of triumph, success, and one that usually does not have a happy ending. Hers does. A story that gives hope and inspiration to others, including her thirteen grandchildren and great-grandchildren. An immigrant's story of escaping hardships and poverty. One that spans from Ireland to the United States. A story that encompasses and embodies the American dream in New Jersey. Similar to an indentured servant paying off her passage, she was living in a foreign land not knowing one soul after deciding to give up her most prized possession – a heart-wrenching decision she was forced to make that haunted her for fifty-three years.

"Mum," that's what I call my mother-in-law, Peg, "I won't bother you again about this, but if you'd like me to write your story, I would be glad to. It's a story worth telling. It will be something the family can hold on to. Would you like that?"

She looked at me and I was unsure what she would say next.

"You know, Tom, I've been thinking about it and I think I will. Now that Mickey has passed, I think I can tell the story. I didn't want to relive everything because Mickey was so good to me and we had a wonderful life. I don't know what I will say, but we can try to write the book. When you think about it, it is a pretty good story."

She spoke. I listened, then typed.

This is Peg's story, her good story.

Thomas A. Gorman

2016

Contents

Chapter 1

The File

The black plastic bags of clothes piled up in the living room. He *did* have a lot of t-shirts. Here is one from Ramsey High School that the athletic director gave him when he first got sick. That was twenty-two years ago. How time flies. More clothes to bag up and give to charity. At least someone will make good use of all his clothes.

Each article of clothing brought back a memory – the black tie covered with dice that he wore to funerals and weddings, baggy jeans that fit him well before he lost all the weight, black sneakers that he wore every day, and t-shirts that he wore proudly with high schools and colleges the grandchildren attended.

For such a small house, there were plenty of places to hide things. The closets were full of clothes, boxes, and memories. I opened the first box. It was filled with tax returns from the past dozen years. He did take good care of me that way. I never got involved with our finances, bills, or taxes. I trusted him to take care of it all. I would joke with him as I signed our tax returns each year, "If I go to jail over this, I'm going to kill you." We would laugh together and kiss – another year filed.

The next box had medical bills. So many bills over the years for both him and me. Each bill brought back a memory of sadness but also of hope because we cheated death each time to gain a few more years together.

Another was a white crate with file folders hanging onto the edges. Again, there were some bills and miscellaneous papers in different folders. But there was another folder that contained different important documents. I opened it and found my original passport when I came to America, my USA Certificate of Naturalization, and copies of letters and documents that *she* gave us a few years ago. I didn't remember her giving these to us but there was so much going on at the time. He obviously filed this folder away for safekeeping.

I sat on the bed and thought of the fifty-six years we shared and began reading the documents. That is when I realized that something was wrong. The dates on the documents and letters did not match up to the story I had told for sixty-three years. The memories of a time I had not thought about came flooding back. They were hitting me all at once, but they were too much to process. Emotions of pain and joy came over me like continual waves at the Jersey Shore. I cried holding the papers tightly in my hands. I hadn't cried like that in years.

Exhausted, I collapsed backwards on the bed and fell asleep.

Chapter 2

Prayers, Pigs, and Plans

I was curious, so I blurted out, "Mommy, where do babies come from?"

"They come from the Cabbage Patch, Peg. Ye know that," Mommy responded.

"Is that where my brothers and sisters came from?"

"Jesus, Mary, and Joseph. Aye, out in the field. Now stop asking silly questions and wash the dishes," she snapped. I quietly thought about what she said as I washed and dried the dishes and put them back into the chipped wooden cupboard.

I was told babies came from the Cabbage Patch. Mommy said she went out in the field and came back with a baby she found there. Seemed plausible enough, right? How could I have known thirty years later Cabbage Patch Dolls would be a huge hit in America with sales in the billions?

Mommy and I continued to wash dishes as we usually did each night. She wore her typical attire of one of a few dresses she owned with her well-worn boots. She laced them up upon occasion when she felt like it. Otherwise, the laces hung at the sides and scraped the ground. She was a stocky woman, strong and hardy, who was constantly working. She rarely drank but loved to smoke. Only occasionally did she wear a bra because she felt it was too constricting. Besides, she was always nursing a baby around the house so it would have been just one more thing getting in the way.

We lived in Kyleogue Shinrone, Birr, Offaly, a short bus ride from Roscrea. Roscrea is almost in the middle of Ireland between Dublin and Limerick. Traveling down the paved road, our home was at the end of a hard-packed dirt and stone driveway after coming through the entrance of a low stone wall. There were nine of us living on the right side of a split two-story home. Another family lived on the left. We helped each other out because in Ireland the poor help the poor. Born with green eyes and black hair on April 12, 1937, I was the third child and the oldest daughter. I had two sisters, Nellie and Annie, and four brothers, Mick, Paddy, Jim, and Jack. Well, actually, I had another sister – my twin. But she died when Mommy fell on a rock while working in the fields. The fall gave my twin a good knock on the head and she died in Mommy's stomach. I survived the accident and was born shortly after the fall.

Several of us were born in April, even Mary who arrived much later. We were all born approximately one or two years apart. If my parents were American, I would have guessed they celebrated a little too much every Fourth of July to have had some of us in April.

Also, part of the family was a black dog named Nellie, like my mother and sister. We were not too imaginative with names. Nellie lived outside the stone wall of our property in a Model Ford car that was abandoned years earlier when it was involved in an accident on the road. She came inside to eat dinner and hang around with us but also went outside whenever she wanted. When my sister Nellie was old enough to realize the dog had the same name as she did, I remember her being upset and whimpering, "They had to name the dog after me?"

"Aye," I said. "Now get over it and love yer dog."

Mommy was always having babies. When I was a little older, I realized Mommy did not go to the Cabbage Patch but actually went upstairs to the bedroom to have the baby. She was really one of a kind. When she was ready to deliver, the doctor was summoned to the house. He helped with the delivery and then left. After the birth, Mommy rose up out of bed, dressed herself, and came down the stairs to the kitchen table with the baby. Then we all sat and enjoyed the supper she prepared.

Daddy was a fun-loving gentleman. He was one of the nicest people I ever knew in my life. He wore flannel shirts, a sports jacket, pants, and big black Wellington boots. He wore boots because it was always feckin raining in Ireland. Most Friday nights after work, Daddy rode his bike to Shinrone, a little town a few miles down the road. Other times he biked to Roscrea. He'd say, "I'll see ye in a couple of hours, Nel." That's what he used to call my mother. It was his nickname for Ellen. You'd hear my mother say, "Fine, Dear, just stay out of the water." Then he'd ride his bicycle to town.

After several hours and pints with his mates at the local pub, Daddy rode his bicycle home. If he was drinking in Roscrea, he and his mate, Pat, had a tendency to make a right onto the road home too soon. Since there were no street lights at the corner and it was a pitch black sky unless the moon was shining, Daddy screamed out to Pat, "Turn right," to help him know he needed to turn onto the road home. Pat, himself not being of sound mind because of too many pints, literally made the right-hand turn immediately when told and not onto the road but directly into the river. The current was strong enough in the middle to carry a person downstream. Luckily, Daddy and Pat stayed closer to shore and after a few laughs, Daddy helped his mate out of the river and ended up all wet himself.

However, Daddy also wound up all wet when he rode all the

way home from either Shinrone or Roscrea, up our driveway, and then suddenly made a slight right towards the lazy stream in the back of the house near the well. Many times he was so piss drunk after the pub that he rode his bike into the stream and fell in. It was funny as hell to see him one minute singing and riding his bicycle and the next to be soaking wet in the "bastard stream" as he referred to it.

Mommy, standing by the window with arms folded and shoulders sagging, said, "Leave him there. He'll wake up soon enough."

"But Mommy, he's gonna drown. He doesn't even swim," I said in a worried voice.

"When he gets cold enough, he'll come up." Sure enough, after what seemed like an hour, Daddy walked back to the house, with his bike in hand, soaking wet.

"Daddy, why do ye ride yer bike into the stream?" I asked.

"I don't do it, Peg. The bike does. I mean, sometimes the bike has a mind of its own," he explained.

My parents were a proud folk. Daddy usually kept to himself and was quiet while Mommy did all the yelling in the house. Daddy was a thin man but strong as a horse. He worked hard and was handsome as hell. He wore a hat with a peak all the time and always had a cigarette hanging from his mouth. I can still hear him now, "Hey, Peg! Get my cap." I quickly left and ran to grab his cap and hand it to him. He was bald as a bat and, being the fun-loving man that he was, he sometimes put grass on his head and then his cap to tease us that he did have hair. It actually looked like he had a squid placed on top of his head and we all had a good laugh at his expense.

My parents loved each other. They were very kind and their love carried over to all of us. We didn't have much in the way of material things, but we had love. What else could a family possibly need? We must have been pretty stupid to be so happy in our squalor, but us kids didn't know any better. We laughed every night and had so much fun together. It doesn't really take that much to have a good time, especially when you have nothing.

To heat the house and stove, we used sticks we gathered in the yard and turf. Turf is very common in Ireland. It is composed of partially decayed vegetation and organic matter cut out of the ground. Several times a year, my siblings and I went to the bogs to buy sods of turf, about the size of a brick, by the wheelbarrow. We made several trips at times to get enough sod to last several months. We unloaded the turf into the shed in back of the house. The turf gave off a pungent odor, but it kept us very warm downstairs when burning in the kitchen stove or fireplace and upstairs when burning in my parent's small bedroom stove.

Outside in the backyard we had an outhouse – a wooden shed with a wooden seat above a hole in the ground. There was a bucket of lime to throw a small shovelful into the hole to help with the smell after you did your business. You wanted to get out of there quickly and not linger too long. Years later when the hole was full, it was covered up and a tray was placed under the seat to catch the *shite*. On a weekly basis, when the tray was full of its contents, they were discarded out in the fields or the lazy stream. To avoid going down the stairs and outside in the middle of the night, we peed in a bucket, one for the girls and another for the boys; my parents had their own. If you had to do something other than pee, you went outside, got wet if it was raining, and did what you went out there to do quickly. Each morning it was someone's unenviable job to empty the buckets.

When we came home from school, I began preparing supper. My job was to make Irish soda bread. I made at least six Irish soda bread loaves every feckin day. That's what we lived on. So when people asked me over the years to make the bread for St. Patrick's Day or other occasions, I replied "Absolutely not" since I was so tired of making it in my youth. The bread was our little snack. We smeared butter, and some jam on a rare occasion, on the bread.

We had some pigs in the yard. When they were plump and ready, Daddy killed them and brought them into the kitchen to be prepared for meals. On a good night, we ate pig's head for supper. Pig's head was one of the nicer parts of the food we fought over. It was eerie when the head was cooking in the pot – it stared at you. Even though I fought over it, I could never eat it, but my brother Jack loved it.

On most nights for supper, we brought in whatever we had out in the yard. We picked the tails of carrots or onions from the field. We brought the vegetables in, washed them, cooked them on the stove, and then ate them. Some mornings when we needed meat with the meal, Daddy shot rabbits in the field with his shotgun from the upstairs window. On a good day, he shot a cock pheasant. But his best shot was when he went hunting in the fields and nailed a rabbit. However, upon closer inspection there were two dead rabbits. It turned out that the slug went right through the first one and hit a second one that was behind the first. We actually ate quite well because Daddy was a good shot.

Next to the kitchen was the pantry or cold room. We stored everything on the floor that needed to be kept cold, such as milk and butter. In the middle of the kitchen was a long wooden table where we all sat, laughed, and prayed. This was the same table my parents would be laid out upon when they died. We said grace before every meal. We all took turns, but Daddy said most of them. He looked up at the ceiling with the hat on his head and said a simple prayer, "Thank God for everything. Thank God for our health and please be good to our kids. Thank ye, God! Amen."

At the table we mostly spoke about what occurred during the day. My siblings and I used to kid around, but there were never any deep conversations about politics or what we wanted to accomplish in life. My parents pretty much left it up to us to figure out our own problems.

Once in a while we pushed the limits. Jim snickered at Daddy and said, "Hey Jim, pass the bread, please." I followed along, "Aye, Nel, can I have some potatoes?" Mommy quickly reprimanded us, "We are yer Mommy and Daddy. Ye don't call us 'Jim' and 'Nel.' Show some respect." We chuckled a little, except Mommy.

Sometimes after supper when everything was cleaned up and put away, we said our own prayers and if Daddy wanted to say an extra prayer, we all sat down and said it with him. We prayed the Lord's Prayer or the Hail Mary. Other times we recited the Prayer of Salvation:

Father, I know that I have broken your laws and my sins have separated me from you. I am truly sorry, and now I want to turn away from my past sinful life toward you. Please forgive me, and help me avoid sinning again...

Other nights, when Daddy was in a singing mood, he lined us up in the kitchen to belt out a song or two. He loved the Irish rebel songs and made sure we knew them all. He was proud of his family and his beloved country. "Everybody line up!" Daddy yelled. Hearing Daddy's commands, we scurried and quickly assembled in front of the fireplace. We stood ramrod straight in a line facing him according to birth order. Mommy joined in too and also stood straight as a stick.

He continued, "Now, all together sing 'The Minstrel Boy.'" Out of key and with all different degrees of loudness, we sang the song like Daddy previously taught us:

The minstrel boy to the war is gone,
In the ranks of death you'll find him;

23

His father's sword he has girded on,
And his wild harp slung behind him;
"Land of Song!" said the warrior bard,
"Though all the world betrays thee,
One sword, at least, thy rights shall guard,
One faithful harp shall praise thee!"

"Good! Now, let's finish up with the 'Wild Colonial Boy.' I want to hear ye good and loud. Be proud!" We all began:

There was a wild colonial boy,
Jack Duggan was his name.
He was born and raised in Ireland,
in a place called Castlemaine.
He was his father's only son,
his mother's pride and joy...
And dearly did his parents love
the wild colonial boy.

Mommy was standing with her arms now folded and Daddy still had his cap on. My parents sang very well. If we were not singing loud enough or did not have our hearts in it, Daddy said, "Did ye forget that? Do I have to teach it to ye all over again?"

Throughout the house, the wallpaper was poorly matched and peeling in many places. Under the stairs connected to the kitchen was a small bedroom where my brother Mick slept until he left for Scotland, and then Jack moved in to have his own room. The other boys slept upstairs in their own room and the girls in another on the left. We shared beds in the rooms. My parents had their own room and shared a bed too. However, to get my own space, I laid a few blankets down on the wood floor to sleep and then Nellie and Annie, who were six and eight years younger than me, had the bed to themselves. Most nights before going to sleep, we played and fooled around usually winding up in my brothers' room. There were battles over the blankets and we kept stealing them from each other.

Jack had a beautiful voice and sang much of the time. When he was a teenager, he accidentally stuck a pitchfork in his foot while working in the field and did not tell anyone. The cut became infected and he ran a high fever and contracted meningitis. He recovered but his hearing was permanently damaged as a result of the infection. Unfortunately for us, this did not stop Jack's love for singing, which proved to be torture for the family since because of his loss of hearing, he was God-awful now.

Upstairs in the bedrooms my brothers shouted, "Jack, shut up. Shut the feck up. Ye don't hear yerself. Ye sound awful. Shut it." My brothers placed a blanket over his head to muffle the noise. But Jack kept singing. You could hear his muffled singing and my brothers screaming, "Shut the feck up! Don't sing anymore!" But this energized him more and he sang louder. No amount of punches from us could stop him. Finally, we figured out we needed to look him straight in the eyes for him to read our lips and once again slowly said, "Stop it. Shut the feck up." My brother Jim was nicer. He wrote down on a piece of paper, "Please shut up."

When Jack was in his sixties, he again experienced a serious health setback. He fell one afternoon and broke his leg. When he went to the hospital, the doctors diagnosed him with septicemia, blood poisoning by bacteria, which left his leg fragile and weak. The poison was traveling up his leg, and the doctors had no choice but to amputate from the knee down. Jack lived his remaining years deaf and with an artificial leg. His feisty attitude did not let these small setbacks slow him down. Jack was tough. He never complained despite these hardships. Hardships were part of our daily lives.

Curious about my future plans in life, Daddy asked me a question. "Honey?"

"Aye, Daddy."

"What do ye want to do in life?"

"I want to go to high school and then university." As he looked at me, he took a deep breath and sighed, "I am so sorry, Peg. Good luck with that."

We knew we needed to leave this place, our home, if we were going to accomplish our dreams. If we stayed, we knew this was certain to be our life forever. My older brother, Mick, already crossed the Irish Sea to find a better life. It did not make sense to stay and be angry about what may have been. I remember my brother leaving. It was not a long good-bye – he just left. I cried at his leaving but was happy he was seeking a better life. I stayed home mostly for Mom because she was tired and working very hard. That was my home until I too had to leave it for good. Another place, another home, another life was calling.

Chapter 3

Trading My Dreams for Corpses

Daddy constantly worked. He had several jobs to provide our meager living. He worked for the county council and for the White Spunners in his spare time. I thought the reason we called them that was because they were white and their last name was Spunners, but it turned out they had a hyphenated or double-barrel name. Mom worked for the White Spunners too. The Spunners, as we called them for short, lived up the road and they owned our property and house. They let us live in our house while my parents worked for them. How else could we have been able to pay the rent? Mommy cleaned rooms inside the Spunners' house, a mansion with several floors. It was a phenomenal dwelling. To make extra money, Daddy sowed wheat or tended to whatever crops were in season for the Spunners when he was not working for the county council maintaining the roads and such.

The Spunners shared everything they had with us. They loved us and were very kind to my family. We were allowed to go to their home and on their grounds to play at any time. They had a beautiful tennis court to match their gorgeous house. The lines on the court were just as perfect as the Spunners were. They were wealthy and we benefited from their graciousness. They owned all the land around our house and all the way up to the monastery. We believe they bought the monastery land years back and their fields were used for hunting and farming. It was like heaven to walk to the Spunners', simply beautiful. We walked about fifteen minutes up the road once leaving our gate to their house. It was right where the bus stop was located.

After school or on weekends we went to their house to play. They had grass tennis courts to play on with my siblings. We didn't know what we were doing, but we had fun hitting the ball back and forth. They also had lovely horses. I loved riding the horses and rode bareback many times straddling the horse. I didn't ride sidesaddle which was more lady-like. At times, we even chased after the foxes in the fields. The horses did not like going over water and they always stopped at the riverbank, where I flew over the horse landing flat on my face. It was not a pretty sight.

It wasn't just the Spunners who had money. *Everyone* did. I had a Protestant girlfriend who lived up the road. She had a gorgeous house too. We spent many a time together and we enjoyed a great friendship, even though we were not equal or the same religion. Money and religion did not separate us; opportunities did.

Usually twice a week, Mommy and I rode our bicycles to Roscrea with a bag on each handlebar to carry some food and house supplies. We'd get bread, milk, meat, and knitting wool at the local stores. We rode the six and a half miles into town together up and down the hills to Roscrea. Most times I couldn't keep up with her. She was so feckin fast on two wheels. My aunt and cousins, the Stapletons, also lived in Roscrea. We typically stopped by their house to say hello. We never stayed late since we wanted to get home before it became dark.

Several times a year, my family gathered together with our cousins and other relatives. Mommy had the seven of us, which was the least amount of children compared to her sisters. The family gatherings were large. When we were older, we'd walk to town to visit my cousins to hang out and play because we were basically the same age.

We never had new things, and we especially never received new shoes. When we outgrew them, we usually were able to get hand-me-downs from a relative or friend. When holes appeared in our soles, we stuffed them with cardboard or newspaper. But they were always polished. Our shoes looked like they were brand new on the outside. On Saturday nights, Daddy made sure our shoes were polished for church the next morning. We shined them up and did whatever was needed so our shoes and clothes were ready in the morning. Truthfully, we only had one outfit that was acceptable for church and we wore it each week. Mommy and Daddy even wore shoes too and not their boots. I don't know if God was looking at our feet in the pews, but Daddy made sure our shoes were shining. He felt a sense of pride knowing we had shiny shoes.

Every Sunday, we walked together about five miles to church. We didn't have a car, so we walked over an hour to arrive at Mass on time. We had the choice of going to 7:00 A.M. Mass at the monastery or walk in the opposite direction for 9:00 A.M. Mass at the church in Shinrone. On rainy days, we ran while the rain soaked through our clothes. To this day, I never remember seeing an umbrella in Ireland.

After walking back home from church, we sometimes watched my brothers play hurling in the afternoon. Hurling, the "warrior's game" as it is known in Ireland, is an ancient Gaelic sport where players use a wooden stick to hit a small ball between the opponent's goalposts. It is a rugged sport and has been the national pastime in Ireland for over 3,000 years. My brothers were good athletes and won several championships with their teams. Jim even made the Tipperary Minor team for players under sixteen. They were tough as nails and had scars all over their bodies to prove it. We all cheered them on whenever they played. On many occasions after games or in the field next to the house, I knocked around with them. I got the best of them from time to time and I let them know it.

As small children, and as soon as we could help around the house, we did our chores and went to school. When we were old enough, we were expected to get a job and bring some money into the house to help pay the bills. We each owned very few clothes, so I only wore two or three different outfits to school during a week. They were always clean. We cleaned them each week by washing them in the sink with a scrub board and hanging them out to dry on the line out back. I also knitted Irish sweaters. In fact, I knitted Irish sweaters for the whole family. When people asked me to knit them an Irish sweater later on in life, I felt the same way as making soda bread and always refused. I was very tired of knitting from my childhood.

I don't remember celebrating birthdays or Christmas. No special gifts at Christmas were exchanged. Maybe we received shoes or clothing because we had outgrown ours or they were totally worn out. But Christmas and Christmas Eve did not have special meaning to me personally until many years later. The holiday did not bring any real change to the day of the week. If the family remembered a birthday, the most we received was a simple "Happy Birthday" and then we went about our day. My parents did what they could with what they had, but it was difficult with so many kids.

Since we couldn't afford private school, we attended the public school up the road. After breakfast, which usually consisted of a slice of bread, butter, and tea, and on lucky days cereal, my brothers, sisters, and I walked about three miles to school. We went through school until the eighth grade and then had to drop out and go to work. Our family needed us to contribute money to the household, so high school was not an option.

The principal of the school was referred to as the headmaster, and the classroom teacher was called the schoolmaster. Arriving on the first day of school, the first task the schoolmaster assigned us was to go into the woods and bring back a stick similar in size to the one he had in the front of the classroom. When each of us returned, we were either commended for following the instructions correctly or hit with the stick that did not follow the schoolmaster's command. As he hit some of my classmates across the back of the legs, he reminded them of the criteria given for the correct stick and sent them back into the woods to find the right one. My girlfriends and I brought back the correct size stick and were not struck with it. The master then had us stand in the front of the room while he used a penknife to slice a flat surface on the thick end of the stick so our name could be written on it and a string attached so it could be hung on a rack behind his desk for future use. If anyone misbehaved in class or consistently gave the wrong answer, the master slowly walked to the rack of sticks, found the name of the student, called the student to the front of the room, and struck him or her across the back of the legs several times. I was so scared of being hit by the stick that I never stepped out of line.

On the way home from school, my siblings, friends, and I passed a large apple orchard that was protected by a high stone wall. Most early evenings, if not all, we took turns scaling the wall to get to the apple trees. The person on the other side picked apples and threw them over the wall to the rest of us to catch. We never had a problem with obtaining our daily piece of fruit. One particular evening, my brother Jim and his friend were throwing apples over the wall as we usually did. When done, they climbed back over the wall and jumped down. When they slowly rose to their feet, they looked up and saw their schoolmaster holding all the apples they threw over the wall. When we saw the schoolmaster approaching us, we all ran. It happened so quickly we didn't have time to warn Jim and his friend. Unfortunately, the master grabbed the two of them, marched them back to school, and used the previously mentioned sticks on them to correct their bad behavior.

My brothers worked at the monastery up the road but received a pittance for trimming the hedges and other odd jobs at the place. I received a scholarship to attend the local high school but couldn't accept it because my mother needed me to help around the house and get a job. I loved school and was quite good at it. I learned the basics of reading and writing, and of course learned Irish, or Gaelic as some refer to it. I read schoolbooks by candlelight in the house since we did not have electricity. At times, Nellie and Annie used an electric torch, or flashlight, that Daddy brought home from the job to be able to read some pages from a book before the batteries ran out within thirty minutes. I loved to read James Joyce. I felt free and alive when I read his works and began to have thoughts of leaving home. I questioned myself, the meaning of life, and what I was going to pursue in life. I knew I could not stay there. I had to break free of that life to pursue a new one. I was a bright person but never had the opportunity to pursue those inner dreams of furthering my education. I thought, *Many years down the road, if I ever have children, I hope they will have the chance to go much further in school than I did.*

Since I was not enrolled in high school, I was able to attain a job as an orderly at Mount Carmel Hospital in Roscrea. Sometimes when I was cleaning rooms, I was called upon to leave my mop and cart behind to assist an aide with carrying stretchers down many stairs to a dark basement. I was willing to work any job as long as I was helping my parents with the bills. I was thirteen. One night while working I wondered, *What's on this stretcher?* I whispered to the aide who I was helping carry the load down the stairs one time, "Do ye have any idea what the feck is on this thing? It's so heavy."

"Don't ye know? These are bodies. Dead feckin bodies," she whispered back.

Shocked, I screamed inside my head, *What the hell are we*

doing here?

I was cold and my hands were clammy all of a sudden. It really scared me that there were bodies on this thing I was bringing down to the basement, which I then realized was a morgue. The aide was in the rear and I was in the front when we carried the stretcher. Since some of the bodies were longer than the stretcher or slid down a little when we went down the stairs, their feet rubbed up against me when we carried them. I can still feel their feet touching my back to this day.

People were dying all the time, so we were busy. It took about fifteen minutes to bring one body down to the basement. That is a long time to be holding death in your arms. It gives a person a lot of time to think about life. Many different thoughts went through my head while carrying these bodies to help me keep my sanity and survive. However, those thoughts were the ones that really bothered you if you let them, especially if you didn't act upon them. After two months, I told Mommy I couldn't do it anymore. She was upset because this meant I wouldn't be able to contribute financially, but she was determined to get me another job. "We'll find ye something, Peg," she said. "Don't ye worry."

At night, Mommy and Daddy tucked us in after everything settled down from all of us fighting and wrestling. They made sure we were in bed all covered up. They didn't kiss us goodnight but they said, "Good night. I love ye."

"I love ye too, Mommy and Daddy." Then we said a quick prayer.

I never felt unhappy growing up. I didn't know any better. Daddy used to hug me and give me a kiss at times and Mommy did too if she wasn't too tired. We knew we were loved. We had nothing, but I knew my parents loved my brothers, sisters, and me. Love is a very great thing – it keeps you sane. That's what I realized as I continually carried death down those dark hospital stairs.

Chapter 4

The Accident

You see, what happened to me was a complete accident.

He was a bit older than me. I met him on one of my errands in town. He was a nice young man who casually flirted with me when I saw him. We never attended school together and there was no dating back then because there were no phones to set something up. We got along well and enjoyed talking to each other during the course of the year whenever we ran into each other. We usually walked and talked about nothing in particular. He was a nice change from doing chores around the house and work. And he made me laugh.

I liked when he chose me to flirt with. It was fun to flirt back, but I made sure not many people could see me doing that. One afternoon, we walked beyond town for some privacy. We sat down and he began kissing me and then, within moments, we were rolling around in the long green grass. After a short while of being in each other's arms, we walked back to town and I rode my bicycle home. We did not say much to each other and I never saw him in town again.

I found myself thinking about that time as the months passed by. I looked for him while I was in town to see if maybe he would flirt with me again or take another long walk. That was my first kiss and I wanted to experience that same feeling all over again. It wasn't him I wanted. I wanted to feel special again.

Seven months later, I said to Mommy, "There's something wrong with my belly."

"What do ye mean?"

"There's all this stuff jumping around going on inside."

Mommy had one of my brothers ask the local doctor to come to the house. A few hours later, the doctor arrived with his black bag. Dr. Doyle was a little man, and he went upstairs to examine me. It hurt like hell. When he was done, he brought Mommy into the room and said, "Nellie, Peggy is going to have a baby."

"I'm going to have a what?" I gasped. I was skinny as a rail and never gained a pound these past few months. "Jesus Christ. I don't understand. I'm a virgin. How can I be pregnant?"

Dr. Doyle looked at me and responded, "I don't know *how* it happened, but *it* happened."

"But, Dr. Doyle, I have never had sex! I swear!"

"Well, you did, Peg. I can see you are confused. Your hymen is still intact, but you are pregnant. That means you had sex and are now going to have a baby."

Mommy was in disbelief too. She said to Dr. Doyle, "I don't understand this. How could this have happened?"

He responded, "You had seven kids, Nel. Why wouldn't you understand? She's pregnant."

My mind was racing. *How could I have gotten pregnant if we didn't have sex? I know we rolled around in the grass that one time. We did press up against each other real close and things may have gone a little further than we expected. Oh, God. What am I going to do now? Jesus, Mary, and Joseph, help me please!*

There were only four options available for a girl in my situation. I could stay at home and have the baby, but that also came with difficulties since both my parents had to work and could not care for me. Having an abortion was illegal and against the teaching of the Church, so that was not an option. Families that had money could keep the matter of their pregnant unwed daughter quiet and hidden by sending her to a private institution. Not liking the first two options, and not having money for the third, my parents figured a fourth option would be the best solution and they began to make inquiries.

Two weeks later, Mommy and Daddy placed me in an unwed mother's home very abruptly. Sean Ross Abbey was a convent run by The Sisters of the Sacred Hearts of Jesus and Mary in County Tipperary. It was known as a "mother and baby home" from the 1930s through the 1970s and was one of the largest of such institutions in Ireland. This abbey sent the second highest number of babies to America for adoption.

In 1921, the two-year Irish War for Independence between the Irish Republican Army and British forces ended, and Northern Ireland, made up of six counties, remained in control of the United Kingdom. The newly formed Irish government deferred to the Catholic Church for help on social issues and institutions while they rebuilt the country. In order to keep Ireland morally pure, unwed mothers were whisked away from society. Since the Virgin Mary was prayed to daily in most Catholic churches and schools, virginity was highly esteemed. Unwed mothers tarnished this moral image that many in Ireland wanted to maintain, and therefore they needed to be hidden. They became "invisible" because their pregnancies and eventual birth of a child contradicted the image of a holy Catholic Ireland.

In 1903, the Sisters of the Sacred Hearts of Jesus and Mary, also referred to as the Chigwell Sisters because they were founded in Chigwell, England, was formed. Their purpose is to bring the love and compassion of the Sacred Hearts to all those they met. One of their principal ministries is the protection and care of unmarried mothers. Their all-white habit, with only their face and hands exposed, and hanging wooden cross necklace matched the stark walls of Sean Ross Abbey.

A monastery was founded on the grounds of the abbey sometime in the sixth century. The main building was a two-storied stone mid-eighteenth century country manor with a basement. Over the years, there were several additions to the original building. The grounds also contained a gardener's house, walled garden, kiln, and several more buildings. The ruins of Corville Abbey were still visible.

The grounds of the abbey were meticulous, green, and beautiful. There were shrines dedicated to Mary and Jesus to pray to in solitude. There was a peacefulness to the place. However, this same beauty coexisted with much death. To the side of the abbey was a small graveyard with headstones for deceased Sisters and an Angel's Plot, where markers identified unwed mothers and babies who died during delivery. There were probably over one hundred markers in this small cemetery, but later investigations indicated the number of babies dying at the abbey to be at least one thousand. Most were of babies that died during birth, but I did see markers of a few mothers, and one who was as young as me.

Sean Ross Abbey was not far from home, about twenty minutes driving distance, and my parents dropped me off with my suitcase containing a few personal items. I was eight months pregnant and celebrated my eighteenth birthday two weeks later, alone, in the cold abbey.

In the abbey there were many girls walking around with babies of all ages, some as old as five or six because their parents never came to take their daughter and grandchild home. They were forgotten and abandoned. This was a problem Irish society did not want to deal with. As a result, we were treated with contempt at best, or invisible at worst.

I was given my own personal room and I stayed to myself mostly because I didn't like the nuns. They were the meanest people – extremely nasty. I cried myself to sleep that night and each night thereafter. As payment for staying there, I was required to contribute and perform many chores around the abbey. I was assigned to make beds, wash dishes, and whatever else the nuns told me to do. Outside, I had to cut the lawn with a push mower and keep the grounds clean. For all this, I was given three meals a day and a bed.

I don't remember one kind nun while I stayed there. The other girls I spoke with told me the same thing. The nuns were not nice or supportive during our most dire time of need. We tried to console each other and shared our similar experiences. Many of the girls thought they were the only ones being harassed. We found a little solace in speaking with each other. The ones I spoke with were younger than me, and they were sad and scared too. I remember I told them my daddy and mommy were going to come back and get me once I had the baby. They said they hoped so because their parents never showed up again. They had been there for years.

The inside of the abbey was spotless and spacious with long hallways connecting many rooms. The mothers were assigned to rooms that had approximately twenty beds. Each mother was given a bed, chair, and small dresser to keep her precious belongings. The few decorations in the sterile white rooms were religious paintings or statues. The nurseries typically held twenty or more babies in metal cribs on wheels. The cribs could be rolled through large glass doors so the babies could get some sun and fresh air during the day. The mothers and babies were kept separated most of the time, but the mothers could visit their babies at different times.

As the babies aged, they were schooled by the nuns in classrooms. Typically, the new mothers stayed and worked at the abbey for up to two years, caring for their child and others who needed help. They were expected to pay off their "debt." If a mother was not welcome back at home and had no other means, she could be sent to one of the Magdalene laundries to learn a "respectable" profession. Unfortunately, many of these "fallen women" as they were known wound up working for free since they had no protections or support system. The term fallen women applied to young girls who lost their good reputation for having sex before marriage as well as to women prostitutes. The laundries were named after Mary Magdalene, the supposed former prostitute who followed Jesus and then became his faithful servant.

Recently, research has tried to educate the faithful that Mary Magdalene was misidentified by Pope Gregory I in 591 during his Easter sermons. Pope Gregory confused Mary Magdalene with the sinner Mary of Bethany who washed Jesus' feet with her tears and dried them with her hair. Mary Magdalene's reputation was sullied after those sermons and stuck ever since. In reality, Mary Magdalene helped Jesus' ministry with her relative family wealth and was considered to be Jesus' closest apostle who was present at His death, burial, and resurrection. She was not the woman of ill repute that many have been led to believe.

Either way, there were an estimated 30,000 women who worked in these institutions. Meanwhile, since the mother was working and living at another location, her baby was taken care of at the abbey until age five or six, at which time he or she could be sent to "industrial schools" that cared for orphaned children. These laundries and industrial schools were often run by religious orders. Other children were sometimes adopted, legally and illegally, by families in Europe and the United States.

I wrote my parents letters, but the nuns checked them so I was never sure whether they got through. I know one did because I told Mommy I had tried to write previously and she responded in a letter,

"Do not worry about it, Honey. We are praying for ye every day."

The delivery of the baby was a nightmare. The nuns left me alone in my room. There was nobody there to hold my hand or take care of me. The nuns couldn't care less. When they came in to check on my progress, they said things like, "Ye must have enjoyed it when ye got pregnant, so now ye're going to sit here feeling sorry for yerself and suffer for yer sins." I responded that my mother and father were coming to see me soon. One nun rebutted, "Oh, yeah. Sure. I've heard that story before. They're not going to come and get ye. Nobody's going to come to get ye."

"Really? Well, I have a feeling my mommy and daddy will."

As she left the room she said, "I've heard that about a million times from the girls who come here. Pray for yer sins or ye'll never be forgiven." Then the door slammed shut.

Pray for my sins? I asked forgiveness from God many times. I was a nice person, hard worker, and loved my family. *Was having a baby a sin? If Jesus was about redemption, shouldn't I be able to be forgiven? Would I be condemned forever?* Agghh! The pain was incredible and quickly banished any thoughts from my mind, except for the thought that I was being punished.

The delivery was further complicated by the fact the baby was breech. I was in labor for many nightmarish hours because of this problem. My punishment continued. Looking back now, I know the baby and I could have died. But there was a nurse who came in to assist me a little. I didn't want anyone else to come in the room because I was fearful they would take my baby away from me. This friendly nurse left for the night, but when she returned in the morning she saw I was still having difficulties.

"You're still here?"

"Aye. Nobody is helping me. I do not know what is going on."

She checked me and realized the baby was breech. She said,

"I will be right back." She ran for another nurse who told me of the problem. *Breech? What does that mean? Am I going to die? Is this my punishment for getting pregnant?* The nurse explained that the baby's feet were where the head was supposed to be and if the baby did not flip, it could not come out and would die. After some time and with much pain on my part, the nurse was able to manipulate the baby to flip, and after pushing for many long excruciating hours, I finally saw a beautiful baby girl born. It was Sunday, April 24, 1955. She was crying and healthy. I called her Mary.

The nurse handed me a light when she left for home and gave me instructions: "If you need my help, put the light on in the window and I'll come back when I pass by." I thanked her. The next night I did put the light in the window and the nurse returned as promised. She helped me so much. She knew I was upset and scared, but she comforted me, saying, "You're going to be alright." I felt better when she told me that. She was the only angel in this place of hell.

Two or three days later, Daddy and Mommy arrived to take me home. One of the nuns came to my room and said, "Somebody's here who says they're yer parents to get ye." I was overcome with joy when my parents came back for me after hearing so many horror stories of abandonment. I responded, "I told ye, Sister." That was the first time I ever called one of the nuns "Sister." I quickly said my goodbyes to some of the other girls at the abbey and wished them luck. One asked whether she could come home with me. I said, "I don't think it's allowed." I have to confess I felt a sense of pride and gloated a little bit as I walked tall past the nuns leaving the abbey and into my parents' loving arms. I was finally getting out of hell with an angel in my arms.

Chapter 5

Certificates

Birth Certificate
Ireland

Date of Birth Place of Birth	Name	Sex	Name and Surname of Father	Name and Surname of Mother	Rank or Profession of Father	Signature, Qualification and Residence of Informant	When Registered
1955 *April* *Twenty Fourth* *Roscrea*	*Mary*	*F*	*-*	*Peggy Holland*	*-*	*Eileen Finnegan* *Occupier* *Sean Ross Abbey* *Roscrea*	*May* *Third* *1955*

CERTIFICATE OF BAPTISM

PARISH OF *Roscrea* DIOCESE OF *Killaloe*
    I HEREBY CERTIFY that *Mary Holland*
was born on the *24th* day of *April 1955* and was
Baptised according to the Rite of the Catholic Church on the *29th* day
of *April* 1955 in the Church of *St. Michael*
by the *Rev. Gerard J. Fitzpatrick*
Sponsor *Kathleen Masterson*
                Signed: Rev. *Patrick Whelan* ~~P.P.~~/Curate
                            Date *25th January 1957*

Chapter 6

Ye Don't Belong Here

When we returned home, we took care of Mary. She was adorable and brought many smiles to our family. Since the time Daddy found out I was pregnant, he began building a high chair and crib for Mary. My parents were very supportive of my situation. They bounced Mary on their knees and sang her Irish rebel songs.

With the used stroller my parents gave me, Mary and I went for long walks because the fresh air is good for babies and knocks 'em out, or at least that's what I was told. I didn't take her to town because it was too long of a walk and I didn't want to take her on the bus. She was too young. However, along those walks, I saw the ugly side of humanity again. I thought I had left hell, but I guess I reentered it. When Mary and I walked past houses of neighbors, some shouted at us, "Bastard child." They were very mean and said such awful things. Others called me "Slut" and "Tramp." When I could not hold it in any longer, I got my back up and yelled, "This is my baby I'm wheeling around here. How dare ye! How dare ye call me names! Ye don't know what happened to me." Other times, if I was in a more peaceful moment, I smiled and answered with a sarcastic, "Thank ye very much. Have a nice day." Once in a while when a woman really pissed me off, I let her know and simply told her to "Feck off."

One Sunday, I decided to take the baby to church with me for the first time. I knew if I entered God's house, nobody could treat me the way people in our town were treating me. How could they? If they treated me like that in the House of God, then they were sinners and God hates sinners. I walked up to the church door holding Mary in my arms and opened the door. A woman standing there inside the door blocked me from entering. I said, "Let me in."

"Ye can't come in here, ye slut. And ye can't bring that 'thing' in here with ye."

"Move aside," I said. "Let me in right now."

"No one wants ye here. Look at what ye've done."

I moved Mary over to my other arm and used my strength to push past this bitch. She couldn't believe I pushed her just as much as I couldn't believe it myself, but this was God's house and I was going in.

There was a small bowl with holy water to bless ourselves as we entered. I reached my finger into the bowl and a man covered it before I could touch the water.

"Excuse me. I'm trying to get some holy water for my baby and me."

"That won't save ye now. Yer not going to get into heaven. Why don't ye leave? Ye're not wanted here."

I looked down at Mary and she was sound asleep. I took a breath and decided to sit without blessing myself with the water. I knew if I sat in the back, I could avoid having many people see me. There was an empty space in the second to last row, and I made my way towards it. As I moved to sit down, a woman, a mother with her five children sitting with her, moved over and blocked my spot. My mouth opened as I began to speak, but nothing came out. I wanted to sit in the front of the church at this point, so the priest could see me and maybe help me with what was going on. But as I turned to make my way to the front, I felt as though every pair of eyes was watching me. It seemed as if everyone had turned to face me; children and adults were snickering, and many were shaking their heads. Mary was still asleep, and I decided to leave and let us both get away from the stagnant air of the church.

There was nonstop heckling over the next eight months. I realized I had to make a decision. I wanted something better for Mary than the life I had been living, so I made up my mind. I was going to have to give Mary up for adoption so she could receive an education and escape this bigotry.

Chapter 7

Please Don't Hurt Her

I came to America because I gave Mary, *my* daughter, away.

People were calling me all kinds of nasty names. I was not just an unwed mother; I was a whore, tramp, slut, and so many other slurs. But they didn't know my situation. I was made of steel. I absorbed all their sneers and comments, but I kept thinking about Mary. She was my first and only priority. *What kind of life would she have living here with this stigma attached to her? She didn't do anything wrong. It wasn't her fault. I have to give her a better life. I wanted a better life for her. I would figure my own life out after that.*

Returning home after a long walk with Mary in the stroller, I said, "Mommy, I'm going to give Mary away and then I'm going to America."

She sighed, "But we can take care of ye and Mary here. Ye don't have to go all the way to America when ye can stay here."

"Naw. Ye won't have to. Ye took care of my brothers, sisters, and me. I want to give her to somebody who's going to provide a better life than I could give her. I can't give her a fair life here."

Her voice was low and trembling, "Whatever ye want to do, Peg, we will support ye," Mommy reassured me.

It was suggested I speak with some people at an agency to help me. Finding out this news, I rode my bicycle to town. At the agency, a gentleman asked if he could help. I blurted out, "I really don't want to stay here anymore. I need to get out of Ireland right now because I'm being harassed."

The gentleman behind the desk said, "Well, you know, we have a service here if you want to get your baby adopted." That took me back. When he said, "adopted," I thought, *Oh, maybe there is a chance Mary can have a better life.* I felt a wave of nervousness, excitement, and relief overcome me all at once.

"Aye, I want her to go someplace where she'll have a good life and get educated." I filled out the paperwork.

A few weeks later, I returned to the agency to meet with four people wanting to adopt Mary. I never interviewed anyone before and was very nervous.

I met with a young couple first. We were brought into another room and we talked for a little while. Next, I met with an older couple. I don't know what it was about them, but I liked them better based upon what they said to me.

I felt bad for the younger couple. They were having a difficult time conceiving and wanted a baby, but I felt since the Timmons couple were older and already had a son, they had experience in raising children. They were warm, gentle, and kind. I liked them right away. I wanted this whole thing to be over with already. When we were done, I told the gentleman I wanted the Timmons to have Mary.

Within the week, with the paperwork complete, Mary and I were able to get a car ride with one of my brothers to the airport. My parents could not accompany me. I left them crying in the kitchen.

For the second time, I met the Timmons as they waited for Mary and me at the gate. I handed Mary over to them.

I said, "Make sure she has an education if it's possible."

Mrs. Timmons said, "Yes, it's possible."

I pleaded, "Please don't hurt her. Please don't hurt her in any way."

"We won't. We will love her very much. Thank you, Peg. I wish you the best."

"I wish ye the best, too. Please take care of this little girl for me. Please."

"We will."

I watched as they boarded the plane to America.

On the ride back home, I cried with mixed emotions of joy for Mary and sadness for me. In my heart, I knew I did the right thing. But giving up Mary was the hardest decision of my life. Mary was gone forever, never to be seen again...or so I thought.

Chapter 8

The Red Hat

I cried every moment of each day for two months after giving Mary up. Was that enough? I prayed to God and the Virgin Mary every night to protect her and forgive me. Now that Mary was adopted and in the arms of a loving family, I knew I had to get out of Ireland. There was no point in staying as there was nothing left for me now. The place that brought me so much joy as a child now only brought me heartache and tears. I turned nineteen and needed to get the feck out.

Ireland is all about connections and knowing someone who knows someone. I had the chance to come to America because I knew the brother and sister of someone living in the New York area who knew of a couple looking for a nanny. Since I practically raised my siblings, I thought this was a perfect job for me. God and the Virgin Mary were finally speaking to me. Having this couple sponsor me was my ticket out.

The Mulligans were my sponsors, and I was to become the nanny and maid for them and their five children. I secured my sponsorship, received my passport, and had found a family for Mary. Not wanting to live in Ireland anymore, I was off to America. Although my parents agreed with my decision to leave, they were brokenhearted. I did what I needed to do for Mary and now it was time I worried about myself.

I was petrified to fly out of Shannon to JFK Airport. This was my first time on a plane and I was leaving home for good. My parents drove me to Shannon Airport. The ninety-minute car ride was quiet. So many thoughts rushed through my head – *Ireland, Mary, my brothers and sisters, America, my parents, Mary, Mary, and more Mary.* I was scared *shiteless.* The only instruction I received was to look for a woman with a red hat when I arrived in America. That was my only connection in this new land: a red hat.

The plane touched down in my new country sometime after midnight. After getting my luggage at the carousel, I found a place to sit and started looking for a woman with a red hat. I was nervous and scared. I didn't dare go to the bathroom for fear of missing this mysterious woman. I couldn't leave; I had no money and had already used my one-way ticket to America. I couldn't return to Ireland. Besides, they probably didn't want me anyway. I waited and prayed.

Hours passed and there was no woman. I said to myself, *Oh, God, where is she? Did they get the right time? Did I land in the wrong airport? Did I make a big mistake coming here?*

Four hours later I saw a woman waddling in my direction. I knew that had to be her because she was the only person here besides me and she was wearing a red hat.

The woman approached me and said, "I'm sorry I'm late."

Sorry ye're late? Bitch. Jesus Christ. Four hours late? I nervously responded, "Me too. I thought I was going to be here forever."

"I am so sorry. I was stuck in traffic."

America must be a busy place to have so much traffic at four o'clock in the morning. I suspected she maybe had a few drinks and stopped for dinner. I finally met my first person in this new country.

The red-hatted woman was named Mrs. Mulligan. She was a

big heavy lady compared to me. I was mostly skin and bones. She was a nice lady. After all, she paid for my flight over to America.

We hopped in her car and drove out to my new home on Long Island, and I met her children and husband who seemed nice enough at the time. Little did I know I was going to have to stand up for myself in this new land too.

The Mulligans had five children between the ages of two and eight, and a few of them seemed to have some type of disability. The oldest, had Down Syndrome; however, at the time she was referred to as a "mongoloid." Her brother was a very nervous child but never officially diagnosed with a disorder or at least they never told me. They lived in a four-bedroom house, and I had my own bedroom. I couldn't stand up straight in it because of the slant of the roof, but I was willing to sleep anywhere. My room was next to the children's rooms.

Mrs. Mulligan worked as a nurse. She also had another daughter, Colleen, from her first marriage, who was the same age as me. Mr. Mulligan was older than his wife and retired now. I didn't get a dime for my labor. Since the Mulligans paid for my flight over here and gave me room and board, I was not paid for my services. I was an indentured servant like other poor Europeans who came before me in the eighteenth century and worked for an employer who sponsored a worker until the debt was paid off. I personally was not fine with the whole situation, but this new life was good enough for now. I was not happy Mary was gone, and I missed my parents and home, but in my heart I knew Mary was in a better place and so was I.

My job was to cook for the family, clean the house, and take care of the five children. The kids called me "Peg" and we adored each other. We had so much fun together. I changed the cloth diapers for the young ones, and after breakfast I put the youngest children in a stroller and walked with the rest of them to the park. At the park, we played on the swings, ran around, and had a lot of fun with some other children who showed up. When it was time for a break, we ate the sandwiches I had made and gave bottles to the younger ones. We typically stayed until four o'clock because fresh air is good for kids – it knocks 'em out. We played the whole day and had a wonderful time.

The first winter after I arrived in America, I remember a quick-moving storm dumped over six inches of snow one February afternoon. It was the biggest snowfall of the year. On the isle of Ireland it rarely snowed and when it did, it was only a dusting to an inch or two. Now, here on Long Island, I was walking in white stuff halfway up my shin and loving it. I bundled the kids up in their winter gear and put bags on their feet before I slid them into their rubber buckled boots. I had nothing, so I went outside with my shoes and bare hands. Some of the children outgrew their old pair of gloves so I improvised. I put socks on their hands to keep them warm. The children and I made snow angels, snowballs, and attempted to make a snowman. It actually looked more like a snow elf than a man. We had a grand time.

When I was able to quickly quiet all the kids down one afternoon, Mrs. Mulligan asked me, "How do you do all this?"

"I just tell them to shut up and listen."

"It's that easy?"

"Aye, it's that easy." I thought to myself, *Ye're a nurse and I'm a nineteen-year-old maid and I'm telling ye how to raise yer kids?*

I liked my new life with this family and felt safe until I came home one afternoon and found myself confronted with my next big challenge.

Chapter 9

My Stand

After working for the Mulligans for almost a month, the children and I returned from the park. Mr. Mulligan was watching TV as he usually did. I went downstairs to do the laundry and all of a sudden, Mr. Mulligan was behind me and I could feel his breath on me. This is not good. I had an uneasy feeling about him since I first met him and felt he looked at me in a peculiar way. Now my hunch was coming true.

He stood behind me for what felt like an eternity. Mr. Mulligan put his hand on my back and moved closer to me wanting something more. So many thoughts went through my head. *I am disgusted by his actions. He knows I previously had a baby and obviously thinks I'm an easy mark - an ignorant Irish girl. This is my home in America and I still did not know anybody aside from the Mulligans. I don't have a penny to my name and have nowhere else to go. I need this job, but I am not going to be anyone's play toy. Am I supposed to let him do what he wants to me so I can keep my job? How the feck will I handle this?*

"Why are ye doing that?" I nervously asked.

"It's okay, Peg," he responded. He slid his hands across my back onto my hips.

"Why are ye touching me?"

"Come on, Peg. Don't be like that." He grabbed me closer and pushed his body against mine.

I was scared. Scared he was going to rape me. Scared if I resisted, I would lose my job. And scared if I told anybody, nobody would believe me. I had an empty, nauseous feeling in the pit of my stomach. I did the only thing I felt I could do in that instant.

A surge of adrenaline ran through my body. I clenched my fists and turned around to face him. Sternly, I stated, "If ye ever put your hands on me again, I will personally beat ye. I will beat the *shite* out of ye."

"You couldn't do that. Come on Peggy, it's alright," he said in a low, calm voice.

"Don't say I couldn't do it because I will. I will beat the *shite* out of ye, tell yer wife and then she will kill ye. Never touch me again," I demanded. He knew I was serious.

He scoffed and backed off slowly. "It's okay, Peg. I didn't mean anything by it. I thought you needed help with the wash." He walked away and back upstairs to his TV as if nothing had happened. My gut told me he may try again one day.

I was scared but proud of myself at the same time. I was furious with him. *How could he do this to me after everything I do for him and his kids?* I never did tell Mrs. Mulligan. In my prayers, I asked the Lord to protect me and to have mercy on his soul. I kept the incident to myself, but I made sure to lock my bedroom door each night when I went to sleep.

This experience, as scary as it was, became a turning point in my life. I realized I was not a scared, helpless person and maybe I never was one to begin with. I saw I was strong and could stand up for myself. I was not a victim and was not going to allow others to dictate my life anymore. I was in America and I was here to stay.

Chapter 10

Time is Growing Near

Catholic Home Bureau
The Catholic Charities
Archdiocese of Chicago

April 30, 1956

Mr. and Mrs. Harry Timmons
Glen Ellyn, Illinois

Dear Mr. and Mrs. Timmons:

In reviewing your application for adoption, I noticed that Mrs. Timmons is over our age limit for the adoption of infants. We do not give out applications to anyone over the age of twenty-nine years. There was possibly some misunderstanding when this application was issued, which I think should be clarified at once. There are several other adoptive plans which we can offer to people who are just barely over the age limit, as you seem to be. I wish you would contact me and arrange to come into the office so that we could clarify this matter.

Sincerely yours,

CATHOLIC HOME BUREAU

By *Bernard M. Brogan*

BMB:hj   Director

My dear Friends,
      We see from your letter just received that
it was posted on the 5th. that is a long time
but I suppose the delay is due to the Christmas
rush,

      You will be glad to know that we have for-
warded a picture of Mary Holland to Revd. Fr.
Brogan of Catholic Charities for your inspection, this is our usual procedure. The picture
has only gone in the last evenings post and
will arraive about the same time as this letter
as there is only one collection on Sunday. If
you call Father he will let you see the picture.
Marys a little Pet and you should be very happy
with her and she with you.

      As time is getting along so quickly we cannot
now hope to have Mary with you for Christmas but
please God you will have her early in the New Year,
her chances for a passport before Christmas would
be only 100 - 1. Of coure if you have got started
on your papers it may work but dont be disappointed.

      We have two children going into Chicago
on the 18th., they are not staying there, just
landing and being met my adopting Parents from
another State.

      P.A.A. [Pan American Airways] will con-
tact you and collect the fare when we have everything ready here. You expenses to this Institution for the preparation of the child will
be $145.00. which will not be paid until you are
sure you are all through.

      Please remember us all in your prayers and
we will pray for you.

      Should it happen that we do not hear from
you between this and Christmas we wish you XXX
every Grace and Blessing and we wish to thank

you for the money for postage, this we think speaks well of your thoughtfulness and makes us feel more happy about little Mary's future. God and Our Lady bless and keep you

Sincerely in the Sacred Hearts.

S R. M. Hildegard

PAN AMERICAN WORLD AIRWAYS SYSTEM
PREPAID TICKET TRANSMITTAL FORM

12-18-56

Total *310.99 US Cy.*

Paid

Issued in favor of: ***Holland/ Mary & Guardian***
Sean Ross Abbey Roscrea County Tipperary, Ireland

Name of Purchaser: ***Harry M. Timmons, Jr.***

January 11, 1957

Sister Hildegard
Sean Ross Abbey
Roscrea
County Tipperary

Dear Sister:

The time is growing near as to when we can expect little Mary to be with us and she will probably be a little surprised to find us with two feet of snow and temperatures below zero. However, we live on top of a hill and I am sure she will enjoy sleding opportunities that awaits her.

I was very glad New Years Day that I had an opportunity to talk to you via overseas phone. The few minutes of conversation put my wife's and my mind at ease, as we did not know exactly when we could expect her.

She seems to have taken over the house already without even being here, with the erection of her bed and items she has received for Christmas from her future grandparents, uncles and aunts. We were rather disappointed, which is understandable, when the 100 to 1 chance did not pay for us so that she could be here for Christmas, but as I write this I realize that it is only a matter of a week or so and she will be in our family.

We pre-paid her flight on the Pan American before Christmas upon instructions to do so from the Pan American. We just wanted to make sure that we would not be the cause of any delay.

We were very much taken with the picture that you sent us of her and my wife claims she favors me, but I can't see it yet.

We hope that all goes well and the final clearances are made in Dublin so that we may expect

her around the time you told me on New Years
Day.

Hoping that our next communication will be one
telling us when to expect her. I remain

Very sincerely yours,

Harry M. Timmons Jr.
Glen Ellyn, Illinois

Dorothy M. Timmons Log

1957

Jan 1st. Harry called Ireland, talked to Sister Hildegarde
We are a little disappointed
Our baby won't be here until after the 21st
11 Harry sent a letter to Ireland
16 Pan American called Mary will be arriving
Jan 26th , 7:20am
23 Miss Corde from PAA called We have refund $112.79
25 La Verne gave me a shower (canasta girls)
26 Picked up our daughter at O'Hare airport 12:25pm
Took Peggy home. Fed her & put her to bed
We were surprised to hear her talk (Airplane Due at 7:20)
Feb 8 D. Schmidt gave a shower for Peggy
April 8 Photo Studio took Peggys pictures - 12 proof
April 24 Peggy Birthday Party

Chapter 11

We Call Her Peggy

February 18, 1957

Sister Hildegard
Roscrea Abbey
Roscrea County Tipperary

Dear Sister:

Mary has been with us now for over three weeks, and I cannot tell you how pleased we are with her. She is everything we expected and more. My son and her have hit it off very well, although now he finds it a little more difficult to do his homework, with her at his elbow.

In Church she behaves like a perfect little lady, although in our Church we have one room set aside, to the side of the altar, which is sound proof and referred to as the "cry room". It gives us a great deal of pleasure the way she behaves, while in church, compared to the other children her age. She displays a considerable amount of initiative and has made herself quite at home. She is quite devoted to my wife.

We had her to our family doctor, for she had a touch of diarrhea, and our doctor said she was in excellent health, but he would be interested in knowing her medical history, particularly what type of inoculations she had already, other than those specified on her papers.

My wife and son and I wish to express our heart filled thanks to you for selecting this wonderful child for us. We have renamed her Margaret Mary and call her Peggy.

Enclosed you will find a New York draft to cover the expenses.
Sincerely yours,

Harry M. Timmons Jr.
Glen Ellyn, Illinois
HMT:jt

1st. March 1957.
My very dear Friends,

Your letter was like a ray of sunshine or a word from Heaven. We were very fond of little Peggy and miss her a lot in spite of all the others we have but she was one on her own in her sweet gentle way. Now it has taken my breath away that you have re-named her - Margaret Mary and are calling her Peggy, this is what her mother was known as and she was one of the most beautiful, gentle, refined girls I have put through my hands, she has gone on for Nursing and is doing well but she is one of the poeple who will always remember the past and be sorry about it.

Now about Mary or Peggy as you call her. She had no Shots except those named on her paper, Diphtheria and Whooping Cough combined and she was as you know Vaccinated. We dont do the B.C.G. except there is a history of T.B. and we have not started Polio shots in this Country as we had only one out-break in my life-time.

What may be giving Peggy the Diarrhea could be fruit, we found she was not able for a lot of Oranges, this brings on loose stools for many of them. When she is a little older she will be able for all such things. Over six months ago she had a prolapse on about four occasions, our Doctor prescribed more heat and less running about for a week or two, it completely cleared so I dont think you have great reason to worry about her. She never had a serious sickness apart from that.

We got the Cheque for which we are more than grateful.

Again my greatful thanks for the lovely letter and for your kindness to Peggy. God and His Holy Mother bless and protect you and yours. Pray for me.
Sincerely in the Sacred Hearts.

S.R.M. Hildegard

STATE OF ILLINOIS
COUNTY CORK

IN THE COUNTY COURT OF COOK COUNTY
October 24, 1957

IN THE MATTER OF THE PETITION OF
HARRY M. TIMMONS, JR. AND DOROTHY

M. TIMMONS, his wife

TO ADOPT

MARY HOLLAND, a minor

DECREE

On this day come the said petitioners, HARRY M. TIMMONS, JR. AND DOROTHY M. TIMMONS, his wife, and this cause coming on to be heard upon the petition and consent of MARGARET HOLLAND, the mother and sole surviving parent of said minor, and upon the consent and answer of GEORGE E. RAMELOW, heretofore appointed Guardian ad Litem of said child and it appearing to the court that the said defendant has had due notice of the pendency of this cause...

The Court further finds that the said MARY HOLLAND, is a female minor of about two years of age, born April 24, 1955 at Roscrea, County Tipperary, Ireland, and that said minor has resided in the home of petitioners for more than six months immediately preceding the filing of the petition herein...

The Court further finds that on January 30, 1956 MARGARET HOLLAND, mother and sole surviving parent of MARY HOLLAND, surrendered her child to petitioners for the purpose of adoption and the Court further finds that said mother has entered her appearance herein in writing, waived issuance of service of summons, consented to an immediate hearing of said cause of action and consented to the adoption of her child by the petitioners...

The Court further finds that the mother and sole surviving parent of said child is of legal age and under no mental disability...

IT IS THEREFORE ORDERED, ADJUDGED and DECREED in accordance with the statute in such case made and provided that from this date the said child, MARY HOLLAND, a minor, shall to all legal intents and purposes be the child of the said petitioners and for the purpose of inheritance and all other legal intents and consequences shall be the same as if born to them in lawful wedlock.

IT IS FURTHER ORDERED, ADJUDGED and DECREED that the name of the said child be and it is hereby changed to MARGARET MARY TIMMONS according to the prayer of the petitioners herein...

29th. December 1957.

My very dear Friends,

It was just beautiful hearing from you again about Peggy. How we have talked of her and her little ways and in spite of all the children we send out no one is ever forgotten and from time to time some particular thing will turn up to remind us of this or that one.

Well we are more than grateful for your most generous gift for the children and I can assure you it will be well and porfitably spent and many a child who does not know comfort will profit by it. I hope God will reward you and increase your own happiness and that of you children.

We had a happy christmas and a lot of that was due to the fact that the children were all well and able to enjoy it and a very great part was due to the good friends who stood to us like you and other generous people. May you all have our prayers and may your reward be very great in this life and the next.

Have you got legal adoption on Peggy, if you have we can give you a new Baptismal Certificate if you need it for school but you will have to send us a copy of the adoption order to keep here in the Church records.

We have a huge number of letters to answer so this will have to finish. God bless you again and again and may the coming year bring you peace and prosperity and every success. Pray for us and we will pray for you all.

Yours sincerely in the Sacred Hearts.

S R. M. Hildegard

for Revd. Mother Superior.

Chapter 12

Mickey

One shining light from this indentured experience was a young woman who I quickly became friends with, Colleen, Mrs. Mulligan's oldest daughter. We first met at her mother's house a few weeks after I arrived in America. She was living on her own and was serious with her boyfriend, Brad. After several visits, she casually asked one night, "Do you want to go out for a beer, Peg?"

"Sure. I don't drink beer, but I'll find something." I had never gone out before in Ireland or America.

I did not drink alcohol on account of the pledge I took when I received the Sacrament of Confirmation. In Ireland, the Pioneer Total Abstinence Association of the Sacred Heart (PTAA) encouraged children to "take the pledge" to not drink or smoke until we were at least eighteen years old, the legal drinking age in Ireland. The PTAA also encouraged devotion to the Sacred Heart of Jesus to help resist the temptation. The Pioneers, as members were known, required abstinence from drinking and smoking for its members but stopped short advocating for a prohibition of these vices. I never had a drop and was not going to start now, but that was not going to stop me from getting out of the house.

Colleen and I hit it off right away. She was easygoing, and we talked, laughed, and had a grand time. We started going out every weekend to the local bars, and I ordered a soft drink or water. She was the only other soul I knew in America outside of the house. We became really good friends.

Eventually Colleen brought along her friend Molly, who was also a local nanny. The three of us enjoyed each other's company very much and had a great time together. One night in a local bar, there was a guy standing next to us talking to Colleen.

"Colleen. That's kind of a funny name. You could be 'Colleen the Bean,'" he playfully suggested.

We laughed and he then turned to me, noticing my heavy brogue.

"What nationality are you?" he asked.

"Irish."

"Well then, that makes you a 'donkey.'"

"Thanks a lot," I laughed. I did not know the Irish were negatively referred to as "donkeys" because they were known for being hard workers and it was cheaper to hire Irishmen than donkeys.

"And who is this other girl?" he continued.

"Molly."

"We'll make you the 'melon' then. So we have 'Colleen the Bean,' 'Molly the Melon,' and 'Peggy the Donkey.'" We laughed, and the nicknames stuck from that night on.

We went out most weekends, and I looked forward to the reprieve from being a nanny, even if only for one night. We danced, drank (non-alcoholic for me), and talked to others at the bars. The bands played Elvis, Sinatra, Chubby Checker, and even some Irish tunes. Once in a while, we journeyed into the Bronx to visit the Kelly Bar.

After a few months, the Mulligans began giving me a few dollars a week for my work. It wasn't much, but I had my room and board covered. Any money I was able to save was spent on the

72

weekends out with my girlfriends or on books, especially books or magazines about Elvis. I loved Elvis.

My room was my sanctuary. When I was done for the evening and the children were in bed, I retired to my room and read or wrote my weekly letters. I missed my parents terribly. I loved receiving letters from my mother letting me know what was going on back home. They warmed my heart. Mom usually started her letters with, "Dear Peggie, Just a line hope ye are all fine we are all in grand Form heare…" Sometimes I received a letter from my brother Jack, which was extra special.

By this time, my brothers had left home and the house was emptying out. Mick had left for Scotland prior to my pregnancy to find work, and I never saw him ever again. He died many years later in Scotland and I didn't even know until six months after the fact. His wife died three weeks after him. They had children, but I never met them. Jim and Paddy went east, in the opposite direction of me, and crossed the sea to England shortly after I left when the Spunners told my parents The Racegoers Club in London was looking for odd-job workers. The Spunners were members of the club but were referred to as the Whites over there. This is where the first half of their family bloodline came from. Jim was fifteen and Paddy a year younger. They worked at the Turf Club at Piccadilly, but the gentlemen's club was not for Paddy. He left in less than a year for work in the construction business, but Jim stayed. He started in the kitchen as a porter and waiter, worked his way up the ladder for over fifty years, and enjoyed a career at the club. Jack, who was deaf due to the infection, stayed around the house until he finally decided to travel to England to work in construction for years. He eventually came back home and stayed in the family house until he died when he was in his seventies.

Jack wrote me a funny story of when he and Paddy were working on a construction site in London. Since Jack was deaf, he did not wear the required ear protection when using the jackhammer. The safety inspector showed up on the jobsite and saw this violation. Enraged that someone defied the mandated orders for ear protection to be worn at all times when operating heavy machinery, the inspector began yelling at Paddy, who was the supervisor of this one project. Paddy, never being one to miss an opportunity to stick it to someone, told the inspector he had warned Jack to wear the protective gear but he didn't listen to him and he should go over and tell Jack himself that it was required.

The inspector stormed over to Jack to reprimand him, thinking he had the upper hand. The inspector yelled, "Hey, where is your ear protection?"

Jack did not respond and kept jackhammering away on the concrete.

The inspector screamed, trying to get his voice heard over the noise of the jackhammer, "Hey, you need ear protection! Put it on or I will write you up!"

By now, Jack could see a man wildly waving his hands in front of him, so he stopped hammering the ground and looked up but did not say anything.

The inspector, truly perturbed now, yelled again, "Get your ear protection on NOW!"

Jack looked at this man, read his lips, and yelled back, "I'm feckin deaf! I don't need protection!" Paddy laughed hysterically at the inspector as he sheepishly walked away to another section of the jobsite.

Not all the letters were heartwarming though. Sometimes I learned of a wedding or funeral back home I was not able to attend, which brought memories of my missed homeland and family. The sense of loneliness intensified at these times. One letter my mother wrote informed me of some of the rumors about me after my departure.

The first was that upon hearing the government was going to take my baby from me because I could not afford to care for the child, Nellie took Mary into hiding to avoid the government officials. This was completely false since I would never let anyone take my baby from me – not the nuns and certainly not a government official. The second was that I left for America while I was pregnant to have the baby. Well, that obviously was not true since I delivered Mary at the abbey after that nightmarish night. The last was that Mary and I both left for America together. That too was untrue since I relive in my mind over and over handing Mary to the Timmons at the airport for adoption.

I am not sure how or why rumors start. Is it that people have too much time on their hands – idle hands are the devil's workshop? Is it that people do not know the truth so they fill the vacuum with what they believe makes the most sense to themselves to complete a story? Or is it that they make up stories to make themselves feel superior to others? I happen to sadly believe the latter is true. I didn't give a damn about the rumors or, aside from my parents, what I left behind in Ireland. I knew the truth and I was living in it every day. The truth was that I gave up Mary for a better life and came to America for a better life of my own. I was not going to let simple-minded folk tear me down or hold me back. My truth now was what was in front of me.

All week long, I was responsible for cooking the meals, setting the table, and cleaning up. I was invited to eat with the Mulligans and celebrate birthdays and holidays but was never truly one of them. Even at Christmas, I did not receive a gift let alone a bonus. When I was with Mrs. Mulligan, our discussions revolved around the children and never delved any deeper. We had a positive relationship, but at the same time it was distant. I was considered the hired help. Maybe if we were a little closer, I would have told her what her husband tried to do to me, but Mr. Mulligan had been keeping his distance so I left it alone.

I was used to cooking and cleaning back home in Ireland. I did it all here too in America and spoiled the Mulligans. When I went shopping, they gave me money to purchase good food. It is easier to make a meal taste good when the ingredients are good. In Ireland, we were just happy to have food on the table.

I knew my way around the kitchen a little, having helped my mother prepare meals for the family over several years. I didn't have any cookbooks to help so I looked at the food and figured out what to do with it. Having formerly cooked chickens and pigs' heads, I knew I could cook the food I bought.

On Sundays, I went to church with Mrs. Mulligan and the children. Each summer, I accompanied Mrs. Mulligan and the children for a long weekend visit to St. Anne de Beaupre in Canada. This basilica is east of Quebec City along the St. Lawrence River. It has been credited by the Catholic Church with many miracles of curing the sick and disabled who visit the shrine there. Each year, we made the pilgrimage and walked up a small mountain to have a priest put his hand on us and bless us. As much as Mrs. Mulligan believed in this pilgrimage, I never saw a change in the children or Mrs. Mulligan.

On the way home, we stopped by Niagara Falls. I stood for a long time along the railing above the river and watched the falls. They were magnificent. I lost myself staring at them and hearing the thunderous roar of the water falling off the cliff. My worries seemed to dissipate and I felt awed by the sense of God. The falls were magical and majestic. I loved seeing the power and force of them. They were breathtaking. They made me feel insignificant and alive at the same time. *How could one doubt God existed?*

Mrs. Mulligan asked, "Do you want to leave now, Peg?"

"No, I am not done yet. I am not ready. It is so beautiful."

One time we went up to the falls in the *Maid of the Mist* boat and I nervously said, "What in God's name am I doing? I don't swim. I am never going to make it back to land. What happens if the boat sinks?" Mrs. Mulligan assured me all was well and the captain was in control.

One year, Mrs. Mulligan treated the children and me to a helicopter ride over the falls. She didn't care to fly herself and asked me to take the kids up in the air. *Who would have thought Peg from Ireland would be flying over the falls?* I was scared flying above the water, but it was beautiful to see God's work from His point of view.

When we arrived home, life continued as it always had. Sometimes Colleen and I went out with her boyfriend, Brad, and on a couple of occasions, he brought along his best friend from high school, Mickey O'Hagan.

The first few times we met, I didn't particularly like Mickey. He was cocky and had a swagger about him. I even told him to his face I didn't care for him and his attitude. He was a piece of work. Yet he was handsome, proud, and very sure of himself. He reminded me of James Dean.

Colleen, nudging me along, said, "Really, Peg? Like you have such a choice. You're going to tell him you don't like him?"

I was afraid to like any man. Thoughts of Mary came to my mind. *How would any man like me, let alone love me, knowing I had a child?*

We met for the first time at Rockaway Beach. There were a bunch of people who frequented the Kelly Bar in The Bronx soaking up the sun, the men in their bathing trunks and the women in their one-piece swimsuits.

Referring to Mickey, someone from the crowd said, "Watch out for this one, Peg."

Mickey replied with a grin, "Yeah, watch out for me."

After our day at the beach, we went back to the Kelly Bar for drinks and dancing. I was shy, but Mickey kept trying to talk to me. I wasn't trying to play hard to get. I didn't think anyone would really be interested in me that way, but he had a look and way about him that made him hard to resist.

At the end of the evening, he asked if he could see me again sometime. I said, "Sure," and that is how we ended the night. No kiss. Not even a handshake.

Colleen and I went back to the Kelly Bar a week later and Mickey was there. Again, we enjoyed ourselves talking and dancing. This pattern continued over the next few weeks. At the end of one evening, Mickey kissed me. I liked it, and I liked him even more.

He said, "Thanks for the kiss, Peg."

"Ye're welcome."

Ye're welcome? I was such a brazen bitch on one hand, but on the other it seemed like I was playing hard to get. Worries about how my past might affect my future with this man made me pull back.

Over the next several months, we continued to meet up at the beach and bars. We enjoyed each other's company very much.

Out of the blue, he surprised me. "Peg, will you marry me?"

"I don't think so," I responded.

I went home that night and said to myself, *Are ye an idiot? This handsome young man wants ye to marry him and ye said no.* Deep down inside I think I secretly loved him from the start.

The next time we met, Mickey and his blue eyes put a little more pressure on me. He said, "Why won't you marry me, Peg? I'm not seeing anybody else and we've kissed a few times. I'm only look-ing at you." I convinced myself his "proposals" were not sincere since they seemed to be said in passing but I felt the pressure for a decision was coming soon.

My twenty-one-year-old self was still hesitant to say yes. A few weeks later, he called the house one night and said, "Hi, Peg, how ya doin? I'm down the street."

Shocked, I said, "Ye're what?"

"I came out here to the little bar in town. Are all your chores done? Can we have a beer?"

I protested, "We're not going out to the Bronx tonight, Mickey."

"No. I'm right down the street. Five minutes. I'll meet you halfway."

I was done with the children and my chores, so I went down to the bar to meet him. We had a wonderful evening.

Mickey said to me, "You know, I think you should stop that babysitting job. You're too good for that. You can't be doing this the rest of your life."

He then said, "Excuse me one minute. I have to make a phone call." He left me with my thoughts. *Can I really leave the Mulligans? I have been working for them for almost three years, but I don't have a penny saved. Is it time to move on? Where would I go?*

He returned shortly and said, "I just called my sister, Kitty. She says she has an extra room where you could stay. Then we can talk about marriage again when you're ready." I thought to myself, *How can I get married? He doesn't know about Mary.*

After Mickey first mentioned marriage to me, I immediately wrote to my mother and waited for a response. In her letter, Mommy counseled me, "Before ye get into anything serious, don't start yer new life off with a lie." That's when I decided, when the moment was right, to tell Mickey everything and if he didn't want me after the truth was told then I would just move on.

I decided to follow my heart and move to the Bronx. It was very difficult leaving the children. They were hanging on my arms and legs on my final day. I was heartbroken, but still had faith the future held promise.

Chapter 13

News of the Baby

27th. January 1959.

My dear Friends,

It was just wonderful hearing from you after so long a time, apart from your wonderful Christmas present and you very kind thought in sending it to help the other children for Christmas, it was a real joy to have the news of the baby, she looks really lovely, tall and strong and happy. I am so very pleased that you are so happy with her, you have your reward in this life and you will have it in the next for being parents to God's own wee darling.

Have you had her legally adopted, if you have you could let me have a copy of the adoption order and I can let you have a new Baptismal Cert., she will need that for school later on and it more convenient to get it now than later on as we have many changes from time to time, as a matter of fact we got a new Superior September 1957 and since then all the Sisters in my block have been changed except myself and that is

81

mostly because of the adoptions, since we opened the Schools in California and the Hospitals in Arfica Revd. Mother General made a lot of chamges so as to help all the Convents calling for Sisters.

Again my most grateful thanks for your kind present and you will be remembered in all the prayers of the Community and have a special place in mine.
God bless and keep you all.

Yours sincerely in the Sacred Hearts.

S R. M. Hildegard
for Revd. Mother.

Sean Ross Abbey,
Roscrea,
Co. Tipperary.

23rd. May 1959.

My dear Friends,

It was wonderful hearing all the news, I am still thinking of it. Margart's new Certificates are herewith enclosed and I send two copies so as to save you the trouble of writing for a long time until perhaps she is getting married or going to be a Sister, how very wonderful that would be. We have a very large number of children in Chicago and some more going out very soon. d.v.

We are into beautiful weather now out it was a very hard winter everywhere and the child got everything that was going so we were very busy.

We expect several of the children back to Ireland for holidays this year as we had last year and you have no idea of how we look forward to it. We also live for pictures of the children so when you have one to spare you will remember us.

God bless and keep you and thanks a million for your gift which is greatly appreciated.

Yours sincerely in the Sacred Hearts.

S R. M. Hildegard

for Revd. Mother

Chapter 14

The Bronx

Mickey's grandmother grew up on a farm, and his grandfather came into a little money back in Ireland. He was from County Tyrone in Northern Ireland. He was Catholic in a mostly Protestant and English-controlled county. As the story is told, Mickey's grandfather collected money from many of the Catholic families in the area to help a young woman sail to New York. Not being educated and having few employable skills, she found a job as a cleaning lady with the Bell family who owned several department stores in Manhattan. There were whispers the family was related to Alexander Graham Bell, the Scottish-born inventor credited with patenting the first telephone, but that turned out to be untrue. It was fun to believe that, though. However, the Bells were well off and several years after being employed by them, this young woman came back to Tyrone and repaid Mickey's grandfather with a sizable amount of pounds.

With this money, Mickey's grandfather gave his sons their share to go to university. Being brash and bold, Mickey's father and uncle, however, decided to use this money to sail to America instead. On the day they were packed up and ready to head off to university in

Ireland, they went to the docks instead, bought two one-way tickets to New York and sailed on an ocean liner to America. They only notified their parents after they arrived in New York.

Mickey's mother came from a farm in Ireland and also sailed over to America for a better life. Mickey's parents met in Manhattan, and after their marriage they moved to the Bronx to raise a family. Mickey's mother did not let his father become a cop because, knowing how ambitious he was, he would have wanted to become a police commissioner and she didn't want that. Instead he became a butcher and worked in the neighborhood. He worked long hours and always had a bottle of Irish whiskey by his side to help keep him warm. His father suffered severely with arthritis because he was in the freezer over twelve hours a day working with the meat. Mickey's brother, John, told me once, "I remember going to Yankee Stadium in the summertime with Dad. We were sitting in the bleachers when I heard him moaning because the sun was so hot but felt good warming his bones. He wore a shirt and tie seven days a week and when he removed his tie and opened up his shirt, I saw he had woolen long johns on. He stripped them down to his waist and baked in the sun like he was at the beach." Mickey's mother worked in a ladies' store on Fordham Road. In the beginning, their relationship was great. However, their marriage began to chill over the years and they mostly tolerated each other.

Mickey was born in 1936. He had an older sister named Kitty, Catherine by birth, and a brother named John, who was three years younger. Prior to Kitty being born, his mother lost her first baby in an accident. When jumping on a trolley at a stop along Tremont Avenue, she either lost her footing or her clothing caught something and was dragged by the trolley for a short distance. She was pregnant at the time and shortly thereafter lost a baby girl who was dead upon birth. According to Mickey, that is why Kitty, being the firstborn, was treated like a princess in the house.

Mickey was very proud to be from the Bronx. Living in the borough gave him the edge and cockiness he needed to defend himself in the neighborhood. Just to be a rebel or maybe because he felt an affinity to the many Irish Catholics in Boston, Mickey rooted for the Red Sox. However, the baseball rivalry between the Yankees and Red Sox is very strong. Having Yankee Stadium nearly in our backyard and being a Red Sox fan was literally taking his life in his hands. He liked that challenge.

Mickey grew up in a two-bedroom apartment with one straight hallway, a kitchen, bathroom, and living room. Growing up, the three siblings shared the same bedroom but when Kitty grew older, she moved in with his mother and his father moved into her old bedroom with Mickey. John slept on the fold-up couch in the living room. Mickey's parents paid for the kids to attend St. Simon Stock Catholic School two blocks down from their apartment despite passing a public elementary school on the way. St. Simon Stock Church was where they attended Mass each week. Mass was held in the school basement since a traditional church was not built on this site. After graduating from eighth grade, Mickey was accepted to Cardinal Hayes High School, where Regis Philbin, who rose to fame as a longtime host of *Live! with Regis and Kathie Lee* (later *Regis and Kelly*), also graduated. Mickey never regretted going to school there, but he was hurt he could not play sports since he worked every day after school. He had to work in order to pay for the tuition. After high school in those days, men had to join the service. Mickey went into the Army Reserves and John left home for the Air Force.

When Mickey was younger, there was a playground on the same block as his house. The park was made up of macadam, grass, and a few trees. Mickey and his siblings played in the park, but when the boys were older they started playing in the street. Punchball was a game similar to baseball but instead of using a bat, the batter used his hand or fist to "punch" the rubber ball into play. The parked cars and cars driving down the street presented obstacles to overcome. They were part of the game. On Saturdays, the big guys played basketball on the full-sized basketball court in the park. As kids, Mickey and John ran for sodas. They went to the delicatessen up the street and bought sodas for the older boys who were thirsty. The payoff came when they returned the bottles for recycling and received a few cents profit. When they were older, they worked at various places to earn some spending money.

As a family, they shared fond memories of going out for pizza or Chinese food with their mom upon occasion, and at special times they were given ten cents for ice cream at night. But they learned quickly they could not go to their parents for cash. Mickey remembered asking his father for a little money one time and his father quickly replied he had nothing to give him. Mickey never asked him for a dime again. He always found a way to survive on his own.

The Bronx was primarily made up of Italian, Irish, and Jewish families with a sprinkle of Germans. The buildings with elevators in our neighborhood were where many of the Jewish families lived, while the walk-ups were where most of the Irish families lived. Each group stayed to their streets or sections, but everyone helped each other out when needed.

It was a great time but a tough place to grow up. The boys were in their fair share of fights in the neighborhood, of course. Mickey and John hung out with their own group of friends, but Mickey looked out for John. Once he had to help John out in a fight. Although John could take care of himself, he was in over his head with a larger older boy and needed some help. Mickey stepped in and that kid never bothered John again. Mickey always protected the ones he loved.

Chapter 15

Under the Boardwalk

Kitty adored Mickey. In his eighth grade graduation autograph book she wrote:

> *To My Darling Brother,*
> *May the Good Lord bless you abundantly with Luck,*
> *Love, Happiness & Success.*
>
> *Your loving Sister Kitty*
> *Good luck in your future*

Nine months after first meeting Mickey, I moved to the Bronx to live with Kitty, my future sister-in-law, at 2314 Valentine Avenue. It was two blocks from the Grand Concourse thoroughfare. Mickey was living in an apartment below where he grew up on the fourth floor with his parents. Kitty had moved out after her marriage to live two floors up in the same apartment building. The brown brick apartment building was a six-story walk-up. It was across from Slattery Playground, a little patch of green where everything else was concrete and brick.

    For most of the summer when we were dating, Mickey drove

us on weekends to Rockaway Beach. He enjoyed the beach and the vastness of the ocean. He felt the power of the water crashing upon the sand. When he was young, his parents, who had saved their money all year, rented a room in a multi-floor boarding house for a week or two during summer vacations. His mother stayed with the family all week and his father rode the train to the house on weekends. The houses were very small and everyone had to sleep in the same room. There was a kitchen on each floor of the boarding house, and it was shared by the other renters also vacationing there. Each family had to agree upon a time to use the kitchen. A family was given an hour for supper.

For some reason, Mickey's mother didn't understand how sun lotion worked or, as the boys told it, she cared about her princess more than them. Mickey's mother helped Kitty get dressed each day before school, and on vacation she rubbed sun lotion on her princess in the morning to prevent her from being burned. The boys were left to get dressed on their own for school, and their mother supposedly applied olive oil on the boys at the beach. The boys would wake up the next morning after a full day at the beach with blisters on their legs and back. Because they were so sore, they wound up spending a lot of time in the house the first week of vacation instead of playing in the sand and water. When they were not in bed nursing their blisters, their mother went in the water by holding onto the ropes and their father waded in with the kids on his shoulders to protect them from the waves. Nobody in the family knew how to swim properly.

Having these memories, good and bad, was why Mickey loved the beach. We enjoyed lying on the beach all day, jumping into the water to cool off, and using the public showers to clean up and change into our evening clothes. When it was time for me to get the saltwater off my body, Mickey stood watch outside the public showers and changing room. He said, "I'm going to stand here until you finish showering."

"You better. Then I'll stand here when you shower."

Laughing, he said, "Okay. We are like tinkers." We both laughed. The tinkers were itinerant people who roved around Ireland in their horse-drawn wagons like the gypsies of Europe.

Since we couldn't afford a hotel, Mickey, pointing under the boardwalk, suggested, "Let's sleep underneath there, Peg."

"What for?"

"Not anything you're thinking about."

"I'm not thinking about anything. Why do you want me to go under the boardwalk?"

"Because we can't afford a hotel. Let's bring a blanket and our pillows next weekend and stay over."

"Oh, now we're going to act real cool and be able to say we stayed at the shore for the weekend, Mick?" He smirked back at me the only way he knew how and gave me complete reassurance with his look.

The next weekend we brought blankets, pillows, beer, and whatever else was needed. I reminded him we were not going to have sex under the boardwalk. He replied, "No sex. We won't have sex in the sand." We slept under the stars and boardwalk with our pillows and blankets and enjoyed the fresh salty air. He never touched me and was very protective.

Throughout the summer, other friends from the Kelly Bar also went to Rockaway and we had great beach parties. Many loved our idea of sleeping under the boardwalk and joined us. We used the bathrooms of the local stores and restaurants along the boardwalk. The owners were courteous and said it was not a problem to use their facilities.

There was a joke back then that if you could reach the top of the bar with fifteen cents you could get a beer in Rockaway. No one checked IDs. There was nowhere to keep one if you did since everyone walked around in a bathing suit all the time. There was one main strip, 103rd Street, between the ocean and the bay, which was mostly made up of bars. Having much pride in one's Irish heritage, people gathered by the county they or their ancestors came from and traveled together in packs to different bars. Of course, usually after midnight and many pints of beer, brawls broke out. The police called for the paddy wagons because so many people were arrested at one time.

"Paddy" coming from the Gaelic name for Patrick, Padraig, was sometimes used as a derogatory term to refer to the Irish. Paddy wagons were large vehicles used to transport people who were arrested. There are two theories about where this nickname came from. The first came from the many New York City Irish arrested and transported to jail in these wagons during the Civil War draft riots of 1863. The second referred to the Irish police officers who used the wagons to transport many individuals arrested during speakeasy raids or barroom brawls. Either way, you did not want to find yourself in one on a Saturday night.

Since there were many drunks involved in these brawls at Rockaway Beach, the police threw them in the paddy wagons and then jail for the night. We did not get involved in these brawls, or at least not enough to be arrested, and went under the boardwalk again – our little safe haven. It was like we were trolls living under a bridge.

Chapter 16

Did He Hurt You?

On Sundays, we attended Mass together at St. Simon Stock Church where Mickey went to school. I prayed a lot. We had enough spare change to place a quarter in the collection basket when it came around. We couldn't afford to eat breakfast out after Mass, so we had a leisurely cup of coffee at the local shop and talked about the upcoming week or our future dreams.

Because we lived in the same apartment building, Mickey and I met in the hallway between the floors to be alone. Many times he grabbed me and kissed me. I said, "Your sister's at the top of the stairs. Watch what you say and do." He responded by hugging and kissing me more. We spent hours talking and holding hands on those stairs.

It wasn't easy to stay away from him and he knew it. I told him he had quite an opinion of himself. He responded, "Peg, why do you say that?"

"Because it's true, Mickey. You just think you're 'it.'"

"Well, do you see this face?" he said with a smirk. We laughed together.

But now it was my turn. I hesitated and then asked, "What do you think about me, Mick? Honestly."

He stood up and looked me in the eyes and said, "You're beautiful, Peg. Look at that face. It's the face of an angel."

Hanging out on those stairs was a magical place where time stood still and all the cares of the world did not touch us. Nobody had told me I was beautiful before. Nobody made me feel so strong yet so weak at the same moment. When it was late and we really needed to get some sleep in order to function the next day, Mickey walked me up the stairs to my apartment.

He said, "Do I really have to go to bed, Peg?" Even though I already had a child and wanted desperately to be with him, I had to rebuff his advances.

"Yes, you do. Remember what we said? We agreed to wait. I'll see you in the morning at that corner of the hall. I'll give you a kiss before you go to work."

Most of our conversations were heavenly. Dreams of our future together made the past seem like it never happened. But it did.

One autumn evening, when we had Kitty's apartment to ourselves, Mickey sounded more serious than in the past and said, "What do you think about us preparing to get married?"

I nervously responded, "What?"

"Peg, I'm really going to marry you."

"Well, you didn't formally ask me yet, Mick, did you? You mentioned marriage a few times to me but you haven't officially proposed."

"You know...you know me," Mick quietly responded. He was cute and a little shy. As rough as he was on the exterior, he was very gentle on the inside. "You know how I feel about you."

As he was talking to me, I felt a sense of panic rising because I didn't know how to get married or be married. *Oh, dear God. What about Mary?*

Remembering the advice my mother wrote to me, I had to

tell Mickey about Mary. I took a deep breath, mustered up enough courage, and told him everything. I said, "Well, Mick, I have a surprise for you. I don't know if you'll still want to marry me after I tell you though."

"How bad could it be, Peg?"

I continued without hesitation, "I have a daughter named Mary. I don't know where she is. I gave her away. I will understand if you no longer want to marry me."

"Oh, my God. Did he hurt you?" Mickey, always the protector, was only worried about me.

I looked at him surprised, "Mick, that's all you want to say about this?"

"Yes."

"No, he didn't."

He responded, "That's good. It's alright, Peg. I can't be mad at you. Let's move on with our life and see what's going to come of it. We're going to have a great life together because we both love each other. I don't want you worrying about your Mary. I love you Peg. I still want to marry you."

I was scared because I figured Mickey was going to say, "Well, I am out of here." But he didn't. After the long painful truth was told at Kitty's kitchen table, Mickey only responded with, "Did he hurt you?" I will never forget those words.

With the secret out, I was now fully committed.

"Yes, Mick, I will marry you."

"I will never hurt you."

"I know, Dear."

Mickey embraced me. He never brought up the situation again. Years later, he did confess to me he cried about Mary and did have difficulty accepting the situation, but he never showed it to me.

We were very happy sitting at the table, but then reality set in.

How the hell are we going to get married? We have no money. Oh, my God, I have to get a dress.

Chapter 17

My Dearest Peggie

April 8
Fort Dix Army Base
New Jersey

My Dearest Peggie,

I love you my Peggie so very much, I just can't wait until I'm home to be with you, I need you so very much, I wish I could tell you how much I love you + need you. I don't know what I'd do without you. I'm so bugged up + fouled up right now I don't know what to do with my self. Your birthday is Wednesday and hon I don't even have money to send you a card. I feel very bugged up about it. I love you Peggie so very much I wish so much I could be with you but it won't be long now when we will be together for the rest of our lives. I'm going to love you so much when I get home. I'm not going to let you out of my arms for at least a week + and you better not give me a hard time my skinny Irish Mick.

Well hon John was down this weekend + we had

a few beer together. (He paid for them). It will probably be the last time I'll see him until he comes home if we don't stop on our way home + see him for a couple of hours.

Well hon things are pretty much the same down here, I had a pretty busy day today. It was pretty funny. A General came around today to look the place over + the battery commander was all shook up. He came down to the gun park were we were working today + told me that the general was coming around + when he did to have everyone doing something. Myself + this other guy were filling sand bags + when the general drove by we stopped working + just looked at him like idiots, we didn't even salute him. After he left the battery commander really chewed us out something awful. He really flipped. I couldn't stop laughing + he really bugged up. Well enough for the stupid Army. Hon I am only using one sheet of paper because I'm pretty low on writing paper, no kidding hon. I'm glad I'm only in this army for 6 mos. or I'd really be screwed up. I have to have you near me all the time, it's [the] only time I feel like somebody is when I'm with you. My Love I need your love so much, that's all I'll ever need out of this life is you. I love you, My Peggie, I'll never stop loving you, I want you as my wife so badly I'm cracking up. Hon I'll say goodnight until tomorrow night, Love me My Peggie, always love me, Good Night My Beautiful Princess, I Love You.

Love Always,

HAPPY
HOLLAND   BIRTHDAY   Mickey
XXX   MY
TSTSTSA   PEGGIE - ILY

98

Chapter 18

I Do

Mickey gave me a band like my mother's until he could afford a ring for our engagement. I told Colleen and the girls that Mickey proposed to me. Colleen screamed with excitement, "Are you kidding me? You honestly think he is going to marry you?"

"I think so," I said.

My other girlfriends said, "How the hell did you get him?"

"I don't know. He asked me and I didn't say no. I just needed a little while."

They continued to tease me, "What the hell do you have that we don't?"

I said, "Well, I don't know, Honey, but I have it. And I have him."

Two months later was our first Christmas Eve together. There was no snow but the day was crisp, cold, and a little windy. After we had dinner with his family, we sat on the stairs in each other's arms. Mick pulled a small gift from his pocket and gave it to me. He saved his money and bought me a simple but beautiful necklace. At that moment I could only cry. He said, "Peg, I wanted to get you some-thing that matched your beauty. This is the best I could find. Merry

Christmas." We hugged and cried on those very stairs that we enjoyed each other's company so many times. I was twenty-two years old and received my first real Christmas gift. From that night on, Christmas Eve had special meaning for Mick and me.

Mickey was away a lot in the beginning of our years together. He was now an engineer and traveled across the state of New York working on various building projects. He usually left Monday morning and returned home Friday night. Other times, his assignments were closer to home, which was more enjoyable for us. But during the year, Mickey also had to satisfy his requirements of the Army Reserves. At one point, he had to serve for six months active duty at Fort Dix in New Jersey. To stay in touch when he was away, we wrote to each other. In every letter or card that was exchanged, we always signed off with "HOLLAND" and "ILY." My last name, Holland, became an acronym between us for "Hope Our Love Lives And Never Dies" and "ILY" was shorthand for "I Love You." However, Mickey, ever-being the romantic, always added "TSTSTSA." This stood for, "To Someone Too Sweet To Sleep Alone." This little extra acronym made his extended stays away a little more bearable.

When Mickey was working close to home, he enrolled in courses at Westchester Community College. He eventually earned his associate degree. He also worked odd jobs in New York City to bring in a little money. I found a job at Crest on Fordham Road. It was a small convenience store that sold everything from candy to household items to the people in the neighborhood. I received a regular weekly paycheck and saved as much as I could. Within a month, I was promoted to manager of the store. I had a lot to learn and there were gaps in my education, having only gone to the eighth grade. But at night, Mickey helped me with any of my questions or things I needed to know.

Back at the apartment, I enjoyed a good relationship with

Kitty. She was "tired" most days and stayed in bed much of the time, so I assisted in raising her son. I helped around the house cooking meals, washing dishes, and cleaning rooms, but I didn't want to continue living that kind of life. I left Long Island for a reason and I paid rent to live here.

Kitty and I became friends. We talked a lot and sometimes went out at night. Unfortunately, she had a difficult life. Her husband, Bobby, was not nice to her in many ways and as a result she lost confidence in herself and became helpless. Bobby was never mean to me. I think he was afraid of me. He was a smaller, wimpier guy. At times when he was angry and had a little too much to drink, he grabbed Kitty by the ponytail and pulled her around the room. She screamed and cried out. I yelled at him to cut it out. Eventually he stopped. I asked him once why he did such things and he replied with a sheepish grin, "Because I feel like it." I responded, "Don't ever try it with me because I'll beat the shit out of you." He was a nasty son of a bitch. He came from alcoholic parents, joined the Navy, attended college, and had a good job with IBM when it was difficult to get a job with companies like that. I didn't like him though. He was mean to Kitty and her son and this was something I could never understand.

I lived with Kitty and Bobby for about a year until Mickey and I were married. Even though he lived two floors below, we only saw each other a couple of times per week. Mickey joined a construction company that required him at times to travel to Montreal and sometimes Upstate New York. When he was home, we frequented the Kelly Bar, rode the train to Radio City or Rockaway Beach, and sometimes went to see a movie. Each night I was with Mickey was special. I loved every moment I was with him.

Mickey made me feel like a princess as compared to a maid or nanny as my previous jobs defined me. I thought I was not good enough for him in the beginning, but he helped build up my confidence every time I was with him. When I didn't understand things, he patiently explained the answers to me. He always told me, "Don't you worry about anything. There's nothing going to happen to you if you're with me."

After telling Kitty the news of our upcoming wedding plans, she said, "I can't believe he's marrying you."

I said, "Is that a good thing or a bad thing?"

"No, I mean it in a good way," she replied. "I am happy for you both."

When I think back, it was beautiful. We didn't have sex until we were married because he was afraid I would have some kind of reaction to it.

He said, "No, we're going to wait until we get married."

I said, "I agree but you don't have to always feckin be nice to me. If you want to have a little sex with me, it's okay."

I know he was tempted, but he said we would wait. That was fine by me. This was how we played our cat and mouse game. I knew he was a nervous wreck regarding this matter and so was I. We agreed to wait. He was a very caring person.

The week before we were married we rented an apartment at the top of a six-floor walk-up in the Bronx. It was a beautiful apartment in a very Irish community with three bedrooms, a kitchen, and a living room. We purchased all the furniture and household items ourselves. Luckily, when I was promoted to store manager I made about fifteen cents more an hour.

Of course, I had to get a dress for the wedding. I went to Macy's by myself to purchase a gown. It was times like these I truly missed my mother. After work a week before the wedding, I came home to the apartment and there was a woman sitting in the kitchen having tea with Kitty. I said to myself this woman looks awfully similar to my mother and then screamed, "Oh, my God! It's you!" I must have hugged my mother for half an hour. My mother was the only wedding guest from Ireland. Her flight was a gift from my bridesmaids.

After catching up on so many things we missed in each other's lives, we went shopping to buy my mother a dress for the wedding. She tried on different dresses and came out of the dressing room for me to see if they fit. Then I noticed.

"Mom! Do you have a bra on?" I asked.

"No. I don't like wearing them, Peg. They're too tight."

She did not like to put in her false teeth either. I told her, "Mom, you have to keep your teeth in for my wedding...and you have to wear a bra."

"For God's sake, Peg."

"I'm asking you nicely, Mommy. I am getting married and want you to look pretty."

"Alright. I will do it for ye," she said. Her teeth were uncomfortable and did not fit well in her mouth. God only knows who made them in Ireland.

We finally found a beautiful dress, which I purchased for her. She looked great, and it was probably the best one she had ever owned. But now she needed shoes. The ones she was wearing were too small and beaten up. Her feet were oozing over the sides.

"Do I have to wear shoes, Peg?"

"Yes, Mom. You do. You can't wear your Wellington boots with a dress."

It was very difficult trying to buy her shoes. Nothing was comfortable for her. We kept on laughing with each pair she put on. It was the funniest outing I ever had. Finally, we found a pair to both our liking.

The next stop was the hairdresser. After getting her hair washed and set, I heard my mother say out loud above the noise from the hairdryer, "Feckin heat. I can't stand it!" The woman who owned the store kept laughing at my mother's colorful statements.

She said, "Your mother is so cute!"

I said, "She's cursing and she doesn't want to be under that heat. She's far from cute today." When her hair was done, the last accessory we needed to shop for was a hat. We truly enjoyed ourselves getting Mommy all set for the wedding. Not feeling comfortable in her new fancy clothes, she kept complaining in her Irish way. I finally said, "This is my wedding. It is not all about you, Mommy."

Referring to all the attention and primping she was getting, she chuckled, "Looks like it is, Peg."

"I'm going to get you dressed and you have to wear a girdle." I still can see her face looking at me like I was crazy. "You have to wear a girdle, Mommy. This belly's..."

"What is the matter with my belly? I had seven kids, Peg! Don't worry about my belly." *Now I'm having an argument about her belly. Jesus, Mary, and Joseph and all the saints preserve us.*

After the shopping was out of the way, we toured the city to see the sights. At the top of the Empire State Building, feeling the wind upon her face, she said, "Ah, such a grand breeze." I couldn't get her to leave. She enjoyed being on top of the world too much. "Grand breeze, Peg. Beautiful view." It was feckin freezing at the top in February. When we finally came down, we walked over to Times Square. She loved New York and was amazed by all the cars and lights – such a contrast to Shinrone. We saw a good portion of New York, but Mom was tired. We decided to leave.

As we drove back home, Mom needed the window open for some air. I asked, "What's the matter with you?"

She replied, "I am going through my changes, Peg. I get hot all the time. I was dying at the hairdresser." I didn't realize she was going through menopause. Now it all made sense.

I switched the subject and asked, "Why didn't Daddy come to

America for the wedding?"

"Ye know him, Peg. He's afraid of the water."

"What do you mean he's afraid?"

She said, "He was afraid the plane would go down and we'd drown because he couldn't swim." Funny how he was more concerned about his inability to swim if a plane went down, as if that would be his primary concern. He was a tough man, but he never flew on an airplane.

I said, "Weren't you afraid of that?"

"No. If I went down, I went down. I have lived a good life."

Mommy stayed in one of the children's rooms while she visited. She walked around the apartment with a cigarette in her mouth and let the ashes fall to the ground. She didn't tap the cigarette into an ashtray, and Mickey followed her around the place to prevent her ashes from falling on the floor as much as he could. She asked Mick, "Ye don't mind if I have my cigarette in my mouth?"

"No, I don't," he said. But I knew what he was thinking as he looked at the trail of ashes around the apartment. Out of courtesy, she went outside and smoked some of the time. I don't remember her not having a cigarette hanging from her mouth. Mickey shared with me that Mom was a pretty funny lady.

I said, "She smokes and wants to smoke in the house. Please don't put her out in the cold."

He said, "She chose to do that, Peg."

"I know, Mick. She'll only be here a short while. Please bear with her a little longer."

Besides not caring about her smoking habits, Mom spoke her mind. While living with us for only one week, she noticed and said aloud that Bobby never shut the hell up.

"Mommy, will you keep quiet, please?" I insisted.

"He's short too, Peg," she said.

"Short? Really, Mom? I think he knows it. Mom, you sit there and listen to me. You don't have to talk to him."

During her stay, we also had many beautiful conversations. She told me, "Ye know, I'm very proud of ye. Daddy's proud of ye too."

That warmed my heart. I missed them so much. Holding back tears, I said, "Thank you, Mommy. I love you and I am proud of you and Daddy too. I don't have money to give you to go back with..."

She cut me off and said, "Just be careful, be nice, and be good to Mick."

"That's all you have to say to me?"

"Aye. He's very nice."

True to his word that we would be married within the year, Mickey and I were wed the day before Valentine's Day on Saturday afternoon, February 13, 1960, at St. Simon Stock Church down the street from where we lived. We had a full Mass at 10:00 A.M. It was a clear and cold day – perfect weather for a wedding. I wore a beautiful white gown with lace sleeves, a train, and veil. Mickey looked very handsome in his three-piece morning suit with striped pants. Since I had no male family in America, Bobby gave me away at the altar. I never realized how much shorter he was than me. Mom was right, he was a little man. I had a moment of panic because I was not sure how he was going to remove my veil without a struggle. I quickly bent down so he could remove the veil from my face to help him out. Kitty was the matron of honor, and John, who I had only met a few times before, was the best man. He originally had plans to go to Mardi Gras on his week of leave, but he changed his plans to be in our wedding. Secretly, I think he was a little upset about not being able to go to New Orleans. As we left the church, everyone threw rice at us. I remember how much it hurt getting hit in the face with the uncooked white rice.

The reception was held at a nice place along Fordham Road

near the Grand Concourse. One of Mickey's friends drove us to the hall. Approximately seventy-five people attended the reception and ate sandwiches, salads, and some hot trays of food. The room was decorated and a DJ played music from the '50s and '60s mixed in with traditional Irish songs. We danced our asses off the whole afternoon into the evening. Mom even got up and danced with Bobby. We hired a photographer for the formal pictures of the event and relied on whoever took pictures with a personal camera for all the candid shots. Several people gave me their duplicates and I created a wedding album with them.

We paid for our own wedding and were sweating it out hoping that we collected enough money from the guests to cover the expenses. Although wedding gifts were always welcome, in the New York area it is also customary to give the bride and groom cash to start their life together. Towards the end of the reception, Mick and I went into the basement of the hall to count the money to pay for the event. To get twenty dollars as a gift was a big deal. As we counted, I was very nervous. I said, "Mickey, there is not enough money here." Only one envelope had fifteen dollars. That was the largest amount we received from someone. *This is not looking good.*

"Mick, we're not going to be able to pay this bill and we're going to be put in jail." Mickey had a very great sense of humor. Whenever something funny was said, he had an ability to make it funnier. So he made jokes about our honeymoon being in a prison cell. I was very nervous but laughing at the same time. Luckily, there was barely enough when we finished counting and maybe a little extra to fill up the gas tank for our honeymoon.

It was a beautiful wedding. Everybody danced and felt very happy. The food was good and our friends were there, which was the most important part. Mom had a great time at the wedding. She danced and enjoyed herself very much. She also danced with Mick, which was a special moment. I found out later that despite my warning she removed her teeth because they were making her uncomfortable and stuffed them in her bra. I am glad she at least listened to me and wore one.

The day after our wedding she returned home. It was another crying scene at her departure. Prior to her returning to Ireland and Mick and me leaving for our honeymoon, she gave me one last bit of advice. She was trying to have a serious "mother and daughter talk" about my honeymoon night, but I couldn't understand what she was trying to convey. I said, "Mom, what are you saying?"

"I just don't want ye to be scared on yer wedding night."

"I already gave a baby away for Christ's sake, Mom."

She also gave me advice to always be honest. This was number one on her list. She said, "If ye have a fight, don't go to bed mad." She continued with more little bits of wisdom that moms and dads tell you and ended with, "I hope ye're very happy, Peg, for the rest of yer life."

Her love for me was obvious. Being a consummate mother, she was worried she was going back to Ireland and would not be there for me. She felt since I was just married that I would now need her more than ever. She was even worried that I would get lost in D.C. on our honeymoon. Deep down inside, I think she was scared she would never see me again. Unfortunately, she was almost right. I only saw her one more time in my life.

Two days after the wedding, we drove down to Washington, D.C. with the little money we were able to save for a short but memorable honeymoon. When we arrived and entered the hotel room, we were shocked and surprised to see Mickey's crazy best friend, Larry, sitting on our bed. I turned to Mickey, "Babe, what is he doing here?"

Mick replied, "I don't know, Peg, I came here to get away from him."

Mick said to Larry, "Get the hell out of here!"

"Alright, Mick. Alright. I wanted to say hello because I'm going back in the service this week. I waited after the wedding to talk to you, but missed you."

Mick said, "How did you know where I was?"

"They gave me your number at the desk." Then Larry turned to me and said, "Peg, you looked great in your gown."

I said, "Where were you? I didn't see much of you at the reception."

"I was in the back."

"Really? Well, did you give us an envelope?"

"No."

Mickey jumped in, "Really, Peg? You're going to ask him for an envelope?"

"Well, it would be nice. Every little bit helps."

Mick again said to Larry, "Get the fuck out of the room."

I joked, "He wants to go to bed with us and be in the middle. Larry, did you come to go to bed with me or..."

Mickey was getting a little hot now and snapped, "That's not funny."

I said, "I'm only joking."

Larry said, "No, but I'm leaving now so...goodbye."

"Bye, Larry," I said.

"Get the hell out of here. This is my honeymoon!" Mickey shouted.

Larry said, "Okay, okay, I'm gone." He then came back snickering and said to me, "I really loved your dress, Peg."

Smiling, I said to Larry, "You know, you have some hell of a nerve."

"Get the fuck out," Mickey said. He was furious now.

That night in the hotel room we were finally able to embrace each other the way we had wanted to for so long. Mickey was so kind and gentle with me. I actually said to him, "It's okay if you want to get rough with me. I am not a China doll."

He said, "Alright, Peg, later."

The next two days, we toured D.C. We saw most of the main sites – Arlington Cemetery, the Mall, the exterior of the White House, and much more. I was overwhelmed with the thought of being married, let alone walking around the country's capital. It was beautiful. Not studying U.S. history growing up, I didn't understand the significance of the monuments and buildings, but I had my own personal tour guide to explain everything to me. I can't remember everything Mickey said, but I do remember walking arm in arm and hearing his melodic voice explain the history of a country we were both proud of. When Mickey was not teaching me history lessons, we discussed our dreams, our future, owning our own home, and children. He predicted we were going to have several children. As we strolled down the Mall, he turned to me and asked, "Peg? Do you want to make a baby?"

"Right here, Mick?"

"No, but soon."

"I would love to but not tonight. Maybe tomorrow night, okay?" We didn't know anything about contraception nor could we afford it. We hoped we weren't going to have a baby right away. We laughed.

For two days, we walked for miles holding hands or with locked arms. He continually told me how happy he was that he married me. Randomly, he stopped walking and hugged and kissed me. That's all we did. Once I said, "We're in the middle of the road here, Mick, let's not get killed on our honeymoon."

That night Mickey said, "I'd like a beer, Peg."

"You have the money for one?"

Since money was tight, we skimped on our meals and didn't drink. Mickey laughed in that mischievous way he did. I told him that

I did not think it was funny that this was how we were going to start our life. He just smiled and hugged me.

When Mickey asked me about my dreams, I didn't really have any. I had been living day to day for so long and never truly had big dreams when I was growing up. All I wanted was an education. I told him one of my dreams was to make sure our children received an education. He affirmed that wish. "Peg, our children are going to go to college."

When I look at my grandchildren and all the things they have, I think how wonderful it is because we never had a chance like that in Ireland. I was sometimes sad and angry thinking of the things I missed out on, but I would not change a thing knowing the way things worked out. There is an old saying I am quite fond of: "If we all put our problems in the street and saw everyone else's, we'd grab ours and run like hell."

So what were my dreams? I was living them in my husband's arms at that moment. He was an angel. He made me feel like a princess, and my past life was slowly fading away. When Mickey was dying many years later, we still sat together and felt the love between each other. I told my children not to feel bad about their father dying. I would not be here if it was not for him. My children graduated from high school and attended college. Margaret even earned her master's degree. Their education was one of the biggest accomplishments in my life. As he held me in his arms in D.C., I realized there was another life for me, and it would be a good life.

Chapter 19

Full Citizenship

Everett McKinley Dirksen
Illinois

United States Senate

Minority Leader

June 1, 1960

Miss Margaret Mary Timmons
Glen Ellyn, Illinois

Dear Miss Timmons:

I learned recently from the Commissioner for Immigration and Naturalization that you completed the naturalization requirements under the law and have been admitted to full citizenship in the United States.

Let me join with other officials in welcoming you into the fold of citizenship in this great, free Republic. I am confident that you will prize this high privilege and exercise the responsibilities which go with citizenship. I commend you on your diligence in completing the necessary procedures and wish you well.

Sincerely,

Everett McKinley Dirksen

Everett McKinley Dirksen

Chapter 20

The Kelly Club

The Kelly Bar was the local establishment Mickey and the neighborhood guys liked to frequent. He brought me there often when we were dating, and we had many laughs and memories. It was a typical-looking bar with tables and a jukebox, and it was often crowded, especially on weekends.

Mickey and I looked forward to our evenings at the Kelly Bar. Friends and family surrounded us. However, we were not close with everyone who entered the place. Once, when we were dating, Mickey saw another man he did not know touch my hand at the bar, and his protective instincts kicked in. Mickey strode over and pulled me away from the man and sat me down. He informed me, "When a man starts to talk to you and lightly scratches your hand or your palm, he is saying something more than hello. He's looking for something, Peg, and it's not a handshake."

"Really? I assumed it was…"

He snapped, "Don't let anyone do that to you."

"Well I didn't let him. He just grabbed my hand and…"

"For the love of Christ. Whatever he wanted wasn't good," Mickey said. He was pissed and I kind of liked it that he could be jealous, protective, and loving all at the same time.

Mickey walked over to the guy who grabbed my hand, tapped him on the shoulder, and trapped him in a corner. Very quietly and calmly Mickey spoke to this guy. I couldn't hear what he was saying, but he obviously got his point across because the guy put his beer down and left the club quickly.

Mickey then waved at me to come over and talk in the corner. He had a way of explaining things to me. Coming from Ireland, I was not savvy to the double meanings of American slang and such. Nor did I have much experience hanging out in bars. Mickey stayed close to me at gatherings because people said many things I did not understand. He quietly explained points I missed. He had a way of making the world make sense to me.

Wanting a bigger space to dance, socialize, and a place that was a little more exclusive, one night after a few pints at the Kelly Bar in 1962, the men came up with the idea of creating an athletic social club. Although the club was established mostly for social and drinking reasons, the members occasionally did form teams to play softball and other games against local bars. They drew up the papers and rented a loft on the second floor of a building above an appliance store. Mickey, being very handy from working several construction jobs, built the bar and did many of the renovations needed to make it into a functioning club. There were about one hundred members to start and only men could join. The application was straightforward, but to keep out certain types of people, question #9 asked the applicant whether he fully subscribed to the U.S. Constitution and whether he had ever been a member of any organization on the "Attorney General's List of Subversive Organizations?" Although there were close to one hundred groups on the list, the most notable this question referred to were the Nazi Party, Ku Klux Klan, and Communist fronts. Being strongly patriotic and not having any part of any of these groups, Mickey and John were original members of the Kelly Social & Athletic Association, or Kelly Club for short, and John was on the Board of Directors. Wives and girlfriends were accepted as guests.

On most Saturday nights, Mickey and I now went to the Kelly Club located at 1770 East Tremont Avenue just off the Cross Bronx Expressway in the Parkchester section of the Bronx. That is where our friends went to dance and have a few pints. American and Irish music came from a jukebox or, on some special weekends, a band that played on a small stage in the corner. There were a few older people at the bar, but most of the attendees were our age. Many had gone to Catholic grammar school together, while others were classmates from Cardinal Hayes High School.

To get into the Kelly Club, patrons and guests entered a dark, dingy, narrow staircase off the main road to the second floor. On Saturday nights, it was usually two or three people deep at the bar. It was difficult to get into the place if you arrived late. There was a small dance floor and tables surrounding it. There were at least ten members of the club who were cops, but there was a strict "no firearms" policy. They had to check their weapons in at the bar for safekeeping when they were off duty. Since John was the bar manager for the first couple of years, he was in charge of safekeeping the guns. He figured the best way to keep them away from the guys who were having too many drinks was to wear them around his belt. Sometimes he had six guns hanging around his waist.

If a member *did* get too drunk and out of control, other members had a quick solution to correct his bad behavior. Several of the guys at the bar confronted the drunken member, picked him up, and carried him headfirst to the top of the steep staircase. He was told, "Calm down or you're going down the stairs." Funny thing is it worked every time. Nobody was ever thrown down the stairs, and each violator seemed to change his attitude immediately after staring down a flight of stairs.

No money was exchanged in the club. Members paid dues and had a bar card with their name on it. Every time a patron ordered a beer, it was marked on their card and the member was supposed to pay monthly. The club was usually only open Friday through Monday nights and members could drink all night long.

One evening, John began telling Mickey and me about a girl named Sandy he worked with at IBM on Central Avenue in Hawthorne, New Jersey. You could tell he was smitten with her. He told us, "She works in Production and twice a day drops off paperwork in our computer room and then runs out. My coworkers and I chuckle at that. Anyway, I asked her what she was doing after work and she said that she was going home.

"I tried again another day and asked her out for a drink and she flat out said no. Can you imagine? I am not letting her off that easy. A few weeks later, I told her I had tickets to a play in the city and if she turned me down, I was going to ask someone else."

"Oh, John, you didn't," I said. Mickey was chuckling to himself.

"Yeah, I did, and she turned me down again. The nerve. She told me to have a good time and knock myself out. So I went with Brenda instead." Mickey was laughing out loud now.

John continued, "A few months later we finally met up at a place after work and talked till two in the morning. We hit it off great and she finally got up enough nerve to come visit me here at the Club. She's coming tomorrow night."

"That's grand, John. We look forward to meeting her," I said.

The next night, Sandy came to the Bronx to see the Kelly Club at its finest. The men, as usual, sat with each other or gathered at the bar. My girlfriends and I sat in the same section of the club and Sandy joined us.

"Hello, Sandy. What do you think of the Club?" I asked.

"Oh, my God. This place is wild. Look at it. It's crazy. I never saw people drink like this and carry on like that. Absolutely nuts."

"Would you like a drink?" Mickey asked.

"Oh, no. Thank you. I don't drink. A soda will be fine," Sandy said.

After a few drinks, the boys began retelling stories. John shared, "After my weeklong leave from the Air Force was almost up, Mom told Mickey to drive me back to the base. The next day we drove the Oldsmobile over thirty hours, with a few pit stops along the way, to Lackland Airforce Base in San Antonio, Texas. We arrived the same day I had to report to duty and work.

"Now Mickey had been cooped up in the car for a day and a half and needed to unwind, so he went out with some of my buddies who were off duty. Well, you can imagine what happened next. Mickey flirted with a cute bartender who had on a low-cut blouse. He ordered a case of beer and a few glasses of beer and slipped her a tip between her partially exposed breasts. One of the local guys in this small bar took offense to this and a brawl broke out.

"As the fight spilled into the parking lot, one of the guys attacked Mickey. Mickey punched him in the face and as the guy fell, he slammed the bar door on his head several times. Then another guy came after Mickey, and Mickey did the same thing. He was very surprised it worked twice and chuckled at that. The fight slowed down, and they got out of there to return to the base."

With a big smile on his face, Mickey chimed in, "When John got off duty and caught up with us, we told him what happened. By now, John was ready for a drink and had the great idea of going back to the bar to get the case of beer I had paid for but left behind because of the fight. As we drove back to the bar, the cops were on the roads looking for us and one began to follow me. We pulled over and tried to hide, but the cops came up from behind, shined the flashlight on us,

119

and arrested us. We spent the night in a jail cell.

The next morning, we had to appear in court. The guys from the barracks collected enough bail money for us, but it was not needed since the charges were dropped. We never did get back the beer we purchased." By now we were smiling and the boys were belly laughing and slapping each other on the back.

The Kelly Club hosted an annual picnic at one of the upstate New York parks. About three hundred people attended. Most of the members brought their whole family. We had a grand ol' time eating whatever food and drinks we brought for the day. Beer trucks were ordered and dropped the kegs off in the park. We played the traditional picnic games like the sack race or three-legged race, which usually had several of us falling flat on our face. The egg tosses became a mess but a lot of laughs. There was the traditional softball game, and if the park had the pool open, a lot of drunk people wound up getting wet. As the day wore on, we settled down and sat in the grass or at picnic tables until we sobered up.

Sandy had been in the picture for a little while now, and John invited her to the annual picnic. On the bus ride to the park, everybody kept offering Sandy a drink. The girl who had never had a drink finally said okay and kept sipping whatever mixed drinks were being passed around. Well, after a short while her world began to spin. She made it through the day but on the trip home, with the roar of the bus engine, fumes from the exhaust, and the rotation of the tires, Sandy wound up having her head in a bag vomiting. She was so upset about the impression she left on everyone. Most chalked up the experience to her having a great day.

Chapter 21

My Second Life

When we started our life together, we packed our few belongings and moved several times over a short period. We eventually moved to 2340 Valentine Ave., several doors down from where we originally left, and made this our home for the next ten years. I jokingly told Mickey that we had to keep moving to stay ahead of the law because he kept receiving parking tickets on our blocks for meter violations, parking when there was snow removal, and double parking. This building was five stories and had black fire escapes on the front of the tan brick building. We talked about having babies and ten months later Michael was born. As time went by, I quit my job and had three more children. It seemed as though I always had one on my hip while pushing another in the stroller. But these were *my kids now.*

Michael, Jimmy, and Pat were born about two years apart at the local hospital. However, between deliveries, I also experienced miscarriages. After Pat, I had one baby that I carried for five months who did not make it. We buried her in the Field of Angels in the Bronx. We named our child Baby O'Hagan.

While I was still in the hospital, Mickey brought Baby

O'Hagan to a funeral home near Fordham Road. They held a little service for her before we buried her. He did not want me to have to deal with the services of our dead baby since I was going through so much already. The experience was very surreal because the baby looked so alive when she came out and I wanted to hug her and love her. She was such a beautiful little thing. That was a Sunday.

Although I was not as far along, we lost another baby. Mickey did the right thing again and had the second one buried in the Field of Angels. The other miscarriages I experienced did not require me to go to the hospital and they passed naturally through my body after a few months. With each miscarriage, I believed God had not forgiven me and this was my continual punishment for giving Mary away. It was a heavy burden to carry, and now my children were suffering for my past sins.

Back at the apartment, I made dinner and Mick and I talked about our day. By this time, Mickey was working in Yonkers so he was home every night. Every day, I walked the children to the park with my friends who also had kids of their own. We bought coffee and donuts and yakked away in the park.

Luckily, my sister Nellie came over from Ireland to help me with the family. I told her after I found out I was pregnant with Jimmy, "I'm pregnant again."

Nellie said, "Oh, for God's sake. I'm very busy."

"Well, try and be here." And she did. At least I had someone there for me. She found a job in New York and lived with us. She stayed for ten years.

When I was pregnant with my last child, the baby was quite big. I told the doctor, "The baby better not die because I'm not having any more children, Doc."

Because of my previous four miscarriages and the difficulty I was experiencing again, the doctor gave me several shots of medication to assist with carrying the baby to term. He then placed me on bed rest for several weeks. The doctor said there was a 90% chance I was going to lose the baby.

I was having a difficult time myself leading up to and during the delivery. When the labor pains came on, Mickey rushed me to Jewish Memorial Hospital in Manhattan. I was very sick and bled through the delivery. I felt as though I was in labor for a hundred hours and because the labor was further along, I was not able to receive an epidural. But the doctor's plan of shots and bed rest worked, and Margaret Ellen was born on January 11, 1969, at ten pounds, fourteen ounces, and twenty-two inches long. Because of her size, I had no worries she wasn't going to make it. When she came out, it looked as though she was four months old. People commented when she was in the nursery, "What's that baby doing in there? She looks a month old." Mickey struggled with the idea of having a girl. As soon as Margaret was born, he said, "What am I going to do with a girl?" I responded, "We'll figure it out." She was the most beautiful thing we ever saw. Holding her in my arms with a tear coming down my face, I looked up to heaven, smiled, and said to *God, Thank you for not being mad at me anymore. Thank you for forgiving me.* The next day the Jets beat the Colts 16-7 in Super Bowl III.

When we were released from the hospital, the boys were waiting for us in the apartment. They kept looking into the baby carriage commenting on Margaret's size. My boys were born weighing around seven-and-a half pounds and measuring twenty-one inches.

In the months after Margaret was born, I struggled with postpartum depression. I was tired much of the time and had difficulty thinking about my little babies that died. The only comfort was knowing they were in heaven. Life went on and the doctor gave me medicine to help me feel better. Over time, things improved but I often thought of the babies.

Upon a follow-up visit to the doctor, he advised us not to have any more babies. I chuckled, "Well, that's not...I can't promise that. We have too much fun."

"Peg," he warned.

"Doc, I don't make babies. He does. I just lay there. He makes the babies." The doctor laughed hysterically.

"I'm just saying, Doc."

The doctor, a little Jewish man, then turned to both Mickey and me and sternly said, "I am telling you, Peg, if you have another baby it could kill you."

He then asked, "Any difficulties with your daughter?"

"None. She is wonderful. But she does keep wetting her clothes more than the boys ever did. The diapers don't seem to work well with her."

"Well, Peg, you have a daughter now. You have to double up the cloth diapers at the top and not at the bottom. That will help absorb more of the urine."

Laughing, I said, "Thanks. We've only had boys, and Mick and I are trying to figure all this out."

"Don't worry. You two will figure it out." The doctor was right, we did figure it all out. Maybe not the way someone else would have done it, but we did alright.

Prior to Margaret being born, I had a fallopian tube taken out because it burst and there wasn't much of it left. The operation never truly bothered me though. I put my faith in God and whatever happened, happened. It turned out I had only one functioning tube and ovary when I had the babies. Imagine if I had them both. I would have had nine kids. We didn't really think I would ever get pregnant with Margaret after the operation, but it seems as though Mickey had strong swimmers.

After Margaret, we didn't have any more children although

I did have one more miscarriage. I later had a hysterectomy because of medical problems I was experiencing. Kitty watched the kids during the day, but at the time she wasn't well. My sister helped out after she came home from work. Nellie had her own bedroom, and the kids shared another bedroom. The boys were in bunk beds, and when Margaret came home, she joined them.

Before the children went to bed, we prayed the Lord's Prayer and the Hail Mary, and talked about how to love God and be good people. Mickey was extremely focused on that part of our life. He wanted them to be good Catholics and have a strong education. We went to church every Sunday.

Having a family now only increased my thoughts of Mary and the guilt I felt for giving her away. I continued to pray for her every night. I prayed I did the right thing and I gave her to the right people. I hoped they were treating her well. That was my biggest hurdle I had to get over, worrying about Mary.

Mickey prayed every day too. He prayed that Mary was safe and happy and that I did the right thing. He prayed for me a lot because I was not in a good place at all. I thought, *God, Jesus, my life sucked.* But I was very strong-willed. I wouldn't let it get the best of me. Giving Mary away was the worst thing I did in my life; but it also was the best.

Mickey called Mary our "Guardian Angel." We believed she was always looking out for us. He consoled me, saying I did the right thing, but often I thought back to the time when I was pushing this innocent child around in her carriage and all the terrible things those people – those Irish hypocrites – said to me, never knowing how this baby came into the world. I know in my heart I did the right thing, but it didn't make me feel any better.

With all the guilt I felt, I couldn't even bring myself to a confessional at the church. Nobody except Mickey knew I had Mary;

but everyone back home did. I didn't even tell Kitty until much later on. I dealt with my guilt the only way I knew how – silently.

Even my mother and I did not talk about it. Our letters and conversations revolved around what was going on in our lives. I sent her pictures of her grandchildren, and she let me know what was happening back home on the farm. We never directly addressed the issue.

James and Ellen Holland, and Nellie too.

I grew up living on the right side of this two-family house in Ireland.

127

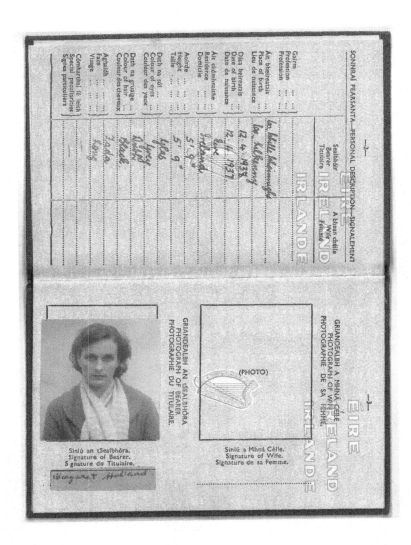

My first passport.

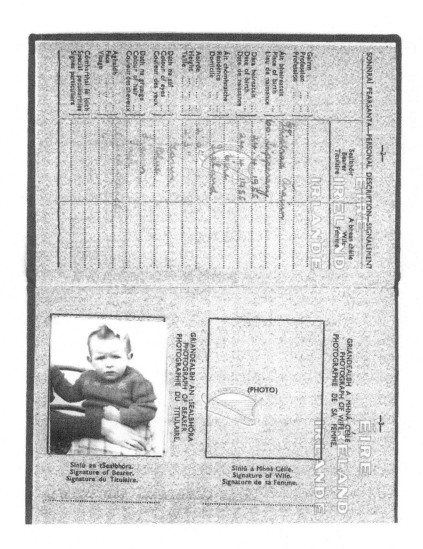

Mary Margaret Holland's passport.

Margaret Mary Timmons' Certificate of Naturalization.

Mary with her father, Harry, and brother, Tim.

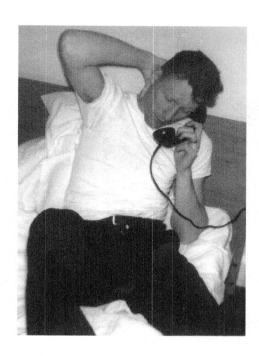

Picture of Mick
when we were dating.

Picture of me
when I was dating Mick.

Mick and I were married on February 13, 1960.

Our early years together.

Ninth Ave. O'Hagan's - Pat, Jimmy, me, Mick, Margaret, and Michael.

Harry, Tom, Meghan, Dorothy, Mary, and Alex.

133

Mary and her mother, Dorothy Timmons.

Mary's search for me brought her to Sean Ross Abbey.

"United" at Newark Airport after 52 years.

Wearing the same green fleece jackets
by coincidence the first weekend Mary and I met.

All the grandchildren at our 50th Wedding Anniversary.

All the children and their spouses at our 50th Wedding Anniversary.

My five children - Pat, Margaret, Mary, Jimmy, and Michael.

The Illinois and New Jersey clans meet up for a Chicago Fire soccer match.

Posing at Carly and Joel's wedding with my two daughters, Mary and Margaret.

Collaborating on the book with Tom.

Chapter 22

In Health...

Although we loved the Bronx, we wanted more of a neighborhood and a house. The kids were getting bigger and the apartment smaller. Also, the neighborhood slowly changed over the years and became more dangerous.

In February of the year we decided to move, Mick and I went out for the evening. Nellie was able to watch the kids. During the evening, a fire broke out on the third floor of our apartment building. We lived on the sixth. Nellie and the kids climbed through a window onto the fire escape to wait for further instructions. After a while, the firemen were able to contain the small fire and allowed them to reenter the apartment.

Two months later, Michael went to the park down the street after dinner. He was probably about nine at the time and saw a fight break out. The fight seemed to be gang-related and unfortunately ended with one of the teenagers stabbing the other in the eye.

As if that was not enough, a month or two prior to us moving, Michael again witnessed a tragedy but this time right in front of our home. A drug deal went down on the sidewalk on Valentine Ave. Something went wrong and one of the guys pulled a gun on the other and fired. The man dropped immediately with a gunshot to the face and died shortly thereafter. Michael was a witness and could identify the shooter but luckily was not asked to do so. We went house hunting on weekends.

After John and Sandy were married, they found a house in Hawthorne, N.J. two doors down from where Sandy grew up on Ninth Avenue. They had two sons while living there. When a house a few doors down from them went up for sale, Sandy's father called Mickey about the opportunity. Mickey almost bought the house over the phone. Hawthorne was also the hometown of Debbie Harry, the lead singer of the band Blondie. Interestingly, she was adopted, raised by a couple in town, and was a classmate of Sandy.

John and Sandy invited us out for a party to their home. On our way out we also looked at houses. We saw one in Glen Rock on Rock Road, but Mickey, growing up with mostly numbers for streets, could not get past the pronunciation of some of the names of the local streets. I told him to focus on the houses, but he got a kick out of many of the street names. We looked at one in Hawthorne we really loved, but it was on The Hill and that section of town was out of our price range.

We wound up buying the two-family house Sandy's father told us about for $26,900, which was more in our price range and it was on a numbered street. We acquired a loan for $19,000 from Boiling Springs Bank to be paid over twenty-five years and moved in at the end of the summer of 1969. So the Bronx moved to the blue-collar town of Hawthorne. Three families of O'Hagans lived on Ninth Avenue – John and Sandy, Mickey and me, and Mickey's parents, who moved in with us in the second floor apartment of our house.

The kids still had their bunk beds. Michael, the oldest, had a captain's bed and even though Margaret had her own room, every morning I found her in a bed with one of her brothers. I said, "You have a bed in there. This is your brothers' room." She said, "I know, Mom, but it's not the same. I have to be with my brothers."

We decided to send the kids to St. Anthony Catholic School in town because we heard the public schools didn't have a very good rating then. We figured what the hell. It wasn't that expensive. It was cheaper in some ways since the children had to wear a uniform and we did not have to spend a lot of money on clothes and shoes.

Mickey did not want me to work so I could raise the kids. Their days typically consisted of a bowl of cereal, jelly sandwiches wrapped in tinfoil for lunch, and buttered noodles with chopped meat, New Yorkese for "ground beef", for dinner. Once a month we went to Burger King. When we drove the two-and-a-half miles to Midland Park for burgers and fries, the kids thought they were in another world and feasting at a banquet. Most nights, we had dinner at the kitchen table with the kids and Mickey said grace. He typically ended the prayer asking God to bless all the children of the world for they were our future. Our children looked forward to time at the kitchen table because if they had a problem or an issue in school, they told us and we talked about it and handled it as a family. We talked about the good and the bad and everything in between. The kids absorbed so much during those discussions. The oval wooden table became the center-piece where we instilled in our children humility, kindness, and love.

We never worried about money, but we never had any either. Mickey religiously played the days of our birth for Lotto Pick 6 at Tony's Stationery Store, but we never struck it big. We didn't go on vacation but were able to take the family down to Great Adventure Amusement Park one Saturday and had a great time together. For Christmas, the children typically received a few gifts that they all shared. At times, payments for the bills, including St. Anthony Catholic School, were late. To make extra money, Mickey built a wooden concession stand next to the town pool and baseball field. We sold hot dogs, hamburgers, french fries, ice pops, soda, and a few other things during the summer months. It was a whole family affair. The money we made helped pay for college tuition, bills, and the extras needed around the house.

Since "The Stand" was small, we cooked much of the food at home and I then drove the hot dogs and other items over to The Stand to sell. The kids worked most of the time at The Stand and complained a lot because all they wanted to do was swim on the hot summer days. Typically, Michael was the short-order cook, Jimmy helped with the grill and dealt with customers, Pat bought and ordered food, and Margaret helped do everything else that was needed. It was all hands on deck. It is true that they lost some of their childhood to work those summers, but they also learned how to work with the public, handle cash, and account for inventory. Most of all, they learned the value of a work ethic and the importance of responsibility at an early age.

On those hot days, Mick did not keep his cool. He was quick to take your order and serve you the food, but he had little patience for indecisiveness or specialty orders. One customer was being particular about his order, and Mickey, not modeling the best customer service, said to the gentleman, "What do you want me to do, eat the burger for you too?" Along a similar vein, a kid ordered a Foxy Ice Pop. Mick either did not know we were now selling these flavored popsicles or did not like weird-sounding names; the result was the same. He snapped at the kid, "What the hell is a Foxy Pop?" The kid did not know how to respond and luckily one of the boys jumped in to serve the stunned customer what he wanted.

Mickey's father passed first and my mother-in-law lived by herself for several years in the apartment. The kids loved visiting their Nana after school and on weekends. They enjoyed a lot of quality time with her. One of her favorite drinks she made for them was homemade eggnog. After Nana whisked all the ingredients together, they sat on

142

the couch to watch professional wrestling. Jimmy "Superfly" Snuka, who was known for jumping on opponents from the top rope in the ring, was her favorite wrestler. She thought he was "dreamy."

The biggest advantage having Nana live upstairs was being able to use her bathroom. Having only one bathroom on the first floor for six people created a line at times. Being able to run upstairs, take care of business, and spend time with Nana was a blessing.

After Nana passed, we rented the upstairs of our two-family home to different tenants. The rent money helped pay the bills, and for the most part we were extremely lucky with the people who lived above us.

As the children grew older, we decided it was time for me to return to work and bring in a little extra cash. My good friend Jo and I opened up a small nook in town called The Hutch that served breakfast and lunch. After a few years, we closed it down and I started a waitressing job at Kirker's Inn. After work, I came home with cash in my pocket from the tips. We called it my "mad money" that I could dip into whenever the kids needed a few dollars.

However, Mickey was the breadwinner. He worked hard in the construction business and worked on projects at the New York Stock Exchange, World's Fair in Flushing, N.Y., and World of Birds at the Bronx Zoo. He had direct association with all of the building trades, as far as layout and engineering, and supervised their work on the projects. Construction in the city was a hard life though. Eventually, Mickey secured a job three minutes from home with the Hawthorne Board of Education as the Supervisor of Buildings and Grounds for all the schools. This kept him local and he was able to enjoy going to work and seeing Margaret in the high school during the day.

After work, Mickey came home and coached the kids in baseball, softball, and basketball. He loved sports and especially coaching baseball and softball. Since he was not able to participate in high school sports because he had to work, he never wanted his children to miss out. His rule for the kids was that sports came before work but definitely after God, family, and school.

On weekends, he fixed up the house with some help from the kids. He removed the paneling, renovated each room one at a time, and built a garage and basement. Underneath the house was a two-foot crawl space. Mickey wanted the basement he never had growing up and applied his engineering skills to accomplish this dream. He used his vacation time with John and the boys to dig out the basement. The crawl space was small and tight, so they had to work on their backs, dig a little dirt, and move it out in buckets. It was dark, dirty, and hard work.

After several weeks and weekends of doing grunt work, John said, "We'll be here forever and freakin' die doing it." He convinced Mickey to rent conveyor belts and two small hand drills. They put the dirt onto the belts similar to what one might see in a mine and improved their digging time considerably. Mickey was driven and once he had his mind set on something, he achieved it. He wanted a basement, so he built one. Eventually he remade the house.

Because of the digging underneath the structure of the house, Mickey had to reinforce the floor beams to keep the first floor strong. He supported the beams with structural poles and told the kids never to touch the pole in the center of the basement or the house would literally fall down. But kids being kids, they played in the basement and eventually hit the pole or swung around on it. Hearing this sound through the floorboards above, Mickey screamed from upstairs, "Don't touch the pole!" for our safety but also probably because he did not want to have the sound of hitting the pole interrupt his watching TV. The command "Don't touch the pole!" is still belted out by one of my children on Christmas Eve to the grandkids playing in the basement.

As the kids aged, the basement became the place for my chil-

144

dren's friends to gather. Sometimes over one hundred people gathered in the cramped dingy basement. Many football victories were celebrated on a Saturday night with the record player blaring in the corner. Because we only had one bathroom in the house, all of the friends had to come up to the living room and talk to Mick and me as they waited on line. We enjoyed our conversations with the kids and seeing them all grow up.

An unofficial tradition began when the boys' friends brought "gifts" to the house and presented them to us. The "For Sale" signs and other lawn ornaments were amusing, but the Lord Jim's Restaurant and Midland Park Police signs went too far. Each Sunday, Mickey returned all the gifts to the appropriate owners but made an anonymous call to the police where they could find their sign after Jimmy dumped it in a nearby baseball field.

We loved living in the "country" compared to the city. As the children grew older, we started having barbeques and parties in the backyard for Communions, Confirmations, and holidays. Each year, we hosted a Memorial Day party that started in the afternoon and went well into the night. Mick's handwritten invitation read:

HEAR YEE, HEAR YEE, HEAR YEE
COME ONE, COME ALL
TO ALL OUR RELATIVES, FRIENDS & NEIGHBORS
YOU ARE ALL CORDIALLY INVITED TO ATTEND
OUR ANNUAL MEMORIAL W/E CELEBRATION.
OUR COOKOUT, EATOUT, DRINKOUT, PASSOUT PARTY
WILL TAKE PLACE.
MEMORIAL DAY SUNDAY
PARTY STARTS WHEN YOU GET HERE.
LOVE YA.
MICK & PEG O

Many of our friends from the Bronx joined us for the day and intermingled with our new Hawthorne friends. As the kegs of beer and food were consumed, many of the gatherings escalated into some pretty wild parties.

For several years, we also joined our neighbors for block parties. To keep the children safe, the police parked cars at either end of the block to prevent traffic from coming down the street, which allowed the kids to play Wiffle ball in the street or our version of "pickleball." Also known as "run down," two players throw a ball back and forth and try to tag the kids before they run to the other base. The kids and adults played this game for what seemed like hours, usually until it was too dark to see the ball being thrown. Knowing the street was blocked off by police cars, allowed the adults to relax and not worry about the kids playing in the street.

Even though there was a town pool, Mickey wanted his own little paradise. He put in an above-ground pool that was only four feet deep, but that didn't prevent my mother-in-law, who decided to go in to cool off on a hot humid afternoon, from getting sunburned and turning into a prune because she was afraid of getting off the raft and drowning. Rationally, of course she could have stood and the water would have only been up to her chest, but a person who never learned how to swim does not think rationally in that situation. Since nobody was home, she had to wait a few hours until I came home from work to help her out of the pool.

When friends from the city and Hawthorne had too much to drink at the parties, many wound up in the pool with their clothes on either because they jumped in or were thrown in. A friend even removed his shoes and socks but left all his other clothes on as he jumped in. Others stripped down to their underwear and went swimming. There seemed to be no rules or decorum.

Jack and Connie were also from the old neighborhood and

moved on the same block as us. One Halloween, they held a party that had a casket on the front lawn as a decoration. With all the Irish present, the Halloween party quickly turned into a Finnegan's Wake, a mock Irish funeral. Someone then put the casket on the roof of a car and slowly drove down the street with the party following, singing and drinking down Ninth Ave. similar to a funeral procession. The coffin was placed on different people's lawns, and friends took turns lying in the casket as toasts and jokes were shared. The crowd then made a right into our driveway and walked the casket up and down with an inebriated friend in it. I am amazed we were not arrested. Probably not the best example to set, but it was a lot of fun.

Chapter 23

Returning Home

Three years after moving to Hawthorne, I decided to return home to Ireland and visit for two weeks. Mickey thought it was a good move. He said, "I really want you to go back home and let your parents see the kids. It would also be good for the kids to see where their mother came from." He could not join us because of work, but I also knew he did not want to go because of what he secretly wanted to do to the man who was Mary's father and the many others who were not kind to me.

This time I was not afraid of flying. I flew the opposite way from which I came and had a round-trip ticket. Just after school let out for summer vacation, we flew out of JFK and landed in Shannon on June 27, 1972. I was excited to see my family and it was wonderful to catch up with Mom and Dad again. My siblings came home from all over to see me. They were working in different parts of Ireland and England, but they made time to return and see their sister. There was a big gathering at the house, and my family was great to me during my visit.

Never having seen much of Ireland myself, my children and I traveled as a family around many parts of Ireland to see the sites. We went to see many of my relatives in the area and also in Thurles,

County Tipperary, Keel, and County Kerry. They all accepted us and were happy we were there. We rode the bus to the different towns, and the kids saw much of the local landscape.

There didn't seem to be any bad blood with anyone. I had no problems being back home. I honestly think people were afraid of me because of some of the threats I made before I left. I ran into many neighbors and schoolmates who were also good to me. When I ran into them, they said, "Oh, Peg, you look grand." Cautiously, I thanked them.

Poor Mommy was afraid something would happen, so she advised me, "Do not yell at them, Peg."

"I'm not going to yell at them, Mommy...unless they say something bad to me."

Again she cautioned, "Just be the better person."

The children slept upstairs in the bedrooms of my old house when they were not jumping on the beds or playing on the farm. One of the days, the boys were mischievous and brought on a little more than they could handle. They wandered up the road a bit and went onto a neighboring farm that had cows and bulls. Whether because of a dare, or out of boredom, they started throwing potatoes they found on the ground at the bulls. Eventually, they hit one who did not like being disturbed from his afternoon meal and charged after them. The boys ran for their lives, but Pat slipped and fell in a cow pie. They were everywhere. Quickly recovering, he began running because of the bull closing in. With hearts pounding, Pat and the boys climbed over the fence and ran all the way home.

Seeing Pat's clothes covered in cow dung and hearing the boys recount their story, I told him to take off his clothes so we could wash them. Since there was no washing machine, my mother walked out back with his clothes and scrubbed them on the washboard. Margaret, being three-and-a-half years old, curious, and wanting to help, asked

150

her grandmother, "Nana, why do we have to wash this cow shit out of the clothes?" Nana stopped washing, glanced at me, and everyone started laughing. Margaret, embarrassed and not knowing why everyone was laughing at her, ran into the house crying.

The boys did not find themselves getting into trouble while playing in the fields all the time though. To help pass the time and keep their skills sharp, the boys brought their baseball mitts, a bat, and a few balls to practice. They asked my brother Jack to hit some balls to them. However, Jack struggled using the American baseball bat, having only played hurling in his life. He asked the kids if he could switch his grip to the hurling style, opposite the way an American batter would hold his hands, and was then able to make contact and send the balls soaring into the sky. The boys ran around the fields shagging fly balls that Jack whacked into the air. The boys were amazed their uncle could hit the balls so high and far with the weird grip, and Jack was equally amazed the boys could easily catch the flying projectiles.

My cousins, the Stapletons, lived near the railroad tracks in Roscrea. Growing up, I always enjoyed their company and this time was no different. We visited them during our stay. To give my children a little taste of the local culture, I thought it was a good idea for the kids to go to the slaughterhouse with their older cousin Willy, who worked there since he was a teenager. Seeing animals prepared for a meal and exposed on tables at the local market for purchase was a common site in Ireland, so I did not think it would be a big deal. Willy met them at the slaughterhouse while I went to town with my mother.

When we caught back up at the Stapleton house after a few hours, the children did not stop talking about all that they saw. They were visibly traumatized by the day. They described their afternoon in vivid detail. They described how they could smell death in the air a few blocks away from the slaughterhouse. They were appalled how the pigs were on an assembly line and chained upside down while the motorized conveyor inched the pigs along. The squeal of the pigs was only silenced when their throats were sliced by the man with the large sharp knife. It was not the afternoon they had expected.

Although school was out, the kids had quite the summer experience learning about another culture. They complained because they felt we walked everywhere and there were many hills. They were exposed to the local butcher, ate rabbit, cooked toast on a long fork in the kitchen fireplace, and swam in the local watering hole that was cloudy and muddy and not like the clear chlorinated pool back home. They talked to their Uncle Jack, who they did not realize was deaf and picked "poppies," slang for potatoes, in the field for meals. They were most amazed at how fast Nana could ride a bike.

The children had the greatest time in the world and Pat didn't want to come home. I said, "I'll leave you here if you don't stop giving me a hard time." He balked and we were able to board the plane. It was a grand trip that I'm glad we took. It was one of the highlights of my life. The only negative was that Mickey could not join us and we missed him very much.

That was the last time I saw my parents. Mommy died at the young age of sixty-five. Mommy was strong, but having so many babies, working all the time, and not having access to proper medical care took a toll on her. I was in America when both of them died and couldn't afford to go home for the funerals. They were laid out on the kitchen table in the house where I grew up.

I thanked Mickey for the trip and when I returned home, there was a used car in the driveway. I didn't know what year it was, but it seemed to be in good shape.

He said, "I bought you a car so you don't have to walk everywhere with the kids." I turned to Mickey, smiled, and once again thanked him for always taking care of us.

Chapter 24

...And in Sickness

It was April 1998, that my Mickey, for the first time in his life, showed a sign of concern. And this time, it was for himself.

We went to The Harp N Bard to celebrate my sixtieth birthday. The twenty-one of us sat at several tables placed together next to the small wooden dance floor. We ate the usual – wings, mozzarella sticks, and nachos for appetizers and cheeseburgers, mac 'n cheese, chicken fingers, and maybe a salad for dinner. While eating dinner, a three-man band came on to play Irish music in the front of the room. Mickey, hearing one of the classic songs, grabbed my arm and asked me to dance. We loved to dance together. There was hooting and hollering from our family as we shaked and shimmied on the floor and Mickey spun me around with his typical dance moves. Some of the grandchildren jumped onto the dance floor and joined in.

"I love seeing you two dance. You are such great partners and move about the dance floor effortlessly," Margaret said to us when we came back to our table.

"Whew," is all I said as I sat down, caught my breath, and took a sip from my Seven & Seven.

"Mommy and I have been dancing together since the Kelly Club," Mick chimed in. "We used to dance for hours." The kids were smiling, happy to be moving around after being cooped up sitting at the table for a while.

Margaret rose out of her chair and hugged her father, who was drinking his beer. As she broke away and gave him a kiss, he turned to Margaret and showed her a bump he noticed on his neck. Lifting his chin and rubbing the spot, he pointed it out to her. She looked quickly, rubbed it, and said, "I'm sure it's just a swollen gland, Daddy."

"Yeah, I noticed the other week when I was shaving. It seems pretty big," he said.

"I'm sure it's a gland thing, but let's go see the doctor to make sure. We'll make an appointment to rule out everything," Margaret said.

Her cautiousness reassured him, but it did not save Mickey from the reality of a tumor living and growing in his neck. A month later, he landed in a surgery room to remove the mass, cutting out over half of his neck. The official procedure was called a left radical neck surgery for a malignancy. Our family waited hours, three to be exact, for him to get out of surgery. Those three hours felt like an eternity, a perpetual ticking of the clock and the anticipation that every shuffle coming down the hallway was the doctor to share the news.

Finally, after we were called in and were able to see Mickey, he looked weak and fragile, just as anyone would after surgery. We waited for him to open his eyes, and when they did, he looked into mine and said what only Mickey could say best, "Peg, did you eat today?" He always worried about me first, then others, and maybe only a bit about himself.

Moving into the summer months, he began radiation treatments at Valley Hospital, a convenient local place where he felt a sense of comfort and familiarity. Mickey was quiet and tough, a mix not many could pull off, but he did. He was the absolute toughest man we knew. If he could tattoo anything on his forehead, it would be,

154

"Get the fuck over yourself."

Margaret accompanied him often for his treatments and learned that even during these awful doses, nothing could affect his durability. The treatments were leaving his mouth full of sores and destroyed his salivary glands. What a nightmare for Mickey. My tough guy left his dentures in the car in the parking lot, and when Margaret and he returned to the car after treatments, he forcibly put his teeth back in, making sure to complete his tough demeanor even facing adversity.

At that time, Margaret and Tom did not have any children yet. When she was not working, Margaret used most of her free time to be with her father who, at this point, lost much of his hair and was looking more frail each passing day. Mickey was resting in our bedroom when Margaret came for a visit in the middle of October, and she could feel the chill both inside and outside. Mickey was not well. She visited with him and sat on the bed to be close to him. She looked at Mickey and held his hand. He could hardly move or open his eyes when she said, "Daddy, I'm pregnant." It was then that Mickey awoke from the tiredness of his fight, opened his crazy big ocean blue eyes, and smiled at Margaret almost as if those words, those few words, had saved him.

Mickey was a fighter his whole life, but some of his toughest battles were with his own body. He fought on the streets of the Bronx to defend himself, fought to win my heart, and fought several internal battles when his body was weakened with coronary disease. Each time Mickey fought, he won. Why would this new battle with cancer be any different? Actually, it wasn't.

He did win his battle against the disease, squamous cell skin cancer, caused by a lifetime of smoking Camel non-filtered cigarettes. However, it was the daily living with a feeding tube connected to his stomach that had to be replaced three times that weakened his body over sixteen years. The radiation treatments destroyed his salivary glands, resulting in his mouth not being able to break down the food he ate. His epiglottis also was compromised and no longer able to prevent food from entering his lungs. As a result, he needed surgery to insert a feeding tube into his stomach so he could pour liquids through the tube to sustain himself. He fought courageously each day living this way and enjoyed many more special moments with his children, grandchildren, me, and eventually, Mary.

Helping their grandfather feed himself became an experience the grandchildren and Mickey shared together. Since most of them were still young, they accepted this way of life about their grandfather and were glad to assist him in the little ways they could. I was deemed his personal caretaker by the doctor since I was trained on how to feed him through the tube. The doctor wrote a letter attesting to this fact, which got us both out of jury duty on three separate occasions. Mickey did not like getting out of jury duty because he considered it an honor and duty, which he fulfilled in the past without hesitation, but his circumstances were different now.

Despite being trained on how to feed Mickey, he would not let me assist him. He was too proud for that. Each day, he conducted his ritual to survive the day. This began with swabbing his mouth with serums and lidocaine, crushing medicine with a mortar and pestle, pouring three cans of Jevity into the feeding tube, inserting the crushed medicine into the tube, and washing it all down with water. This was repeated three times per day. Since Mickey did not need my help, or did not want to burden me, I slipped out of the house when he was sleeping late into the morning because he could never get a full night's rest. I felt guilty having meals in the kitchen when he could not. He was always polite about me eating at home and worried whether I was eating enough, but I had difficulty having meals in front of him. I frequently left to eat at diners and restaurants with family and friends.

The family visited Mickey some nights during the week, but typically on weekends there were more visitors. In fact, his brother, John, made the habit to visit every Sunday afternoon to drink a few Coors Lights and reminisce about the old days. Mickey had a cigarette. These afternoons became something they both looked forward to.

Mickey's body was scarred from fights, construction accidents, and surgeries. When the kids were young, Mickey's intestines were blocked, requiring surgery to correct the issue. He remained in the hospital for a month and lost a lot of weight. Yet he was still allowed to smoke in the hospital bed, and some of the doctors did too when making rounds.

This was the first time I really worried about Mickey. He was the steady rock for me and to see him sick in a hospital bed scared me. The Brudzinskis, our long-time friends who lived across the street, reassured me and commented that Mick had nine lives and that you couldn't take Mick out. As comforting as that thought was, I was still concerned about our four children.

In his forties, Mick was diagnosed with an irregular heartbeat believed to have been caused by a virus. He was on an experimental medication that everyone unfortunately died from except for Mickey and another gentleman who actually died from falling off a ladder. They discontinued use of the drug. Mickey was the lone survivor – a position he was used to.

The physical battles were not all we fought. While we did truly love each other, there were times that presented challenges for us emotionally. In 1987, Margaret was the last to leave for college and for the first time in twenty-five years the house was empty of children. We even lost our beloved German Shepherd, King, who used to play with Mickey on our bed every day when he came home from work. The house was quiet.

To fill the void, Mickey and I frequented The Golden Steer,

Kirker's Inn, and Elks Club – all local Hawthorne establishments. Mickey was a lifelong and proud member of the Elks. We joked that if we had not spent so much money at these places, we probably could have retired earlier. However, we met many of our friends out at these places, ate dinner, had many drinks, and enjoyed many laughs.

Mickey swore off Dewar's Scotch Whisky a few years earlier after a promise he made to the children and me. Mickey's last night he drank Scotch was a bad one. He came home on a Thursday night from the Elks Club lit up and raised the roof in the house with a lot of anger and screaming. The children and I cried ourselves to sleep. The next day he sat us all down at the kitchen table and apologized. Then, he poured his last bottle of Dewar's down the kitchen sink while we all stared in amazement.

Mickey still enjoyed getting a whiff of an open scotch bottle whenever he had an opportunity but never touched a drop. The nights we went out each week were enjoyable and helped pass the time of the empty nest, and when we ordered drinks, Mickey ordered a Coors Light while I ordered either a VO and Club or a Seven & Seven. Alcohol, though, was the drink of the devil.

When we returned home to our empty house, we started getting into meaningless fights. They were usually alcohol-induced. Margaret, when home from college, even commented how she hated Thursday nights because she knew an ugliness ensued. Some of these nights were dark, but our love for each other never wavered.

Throughout his life, Mick made lots of lists regarding various things going on in his life. He meticulously kept files and notes for tax purposes or medical records. He also made goals for himself and us each year that were usually attained.

In his black columnar book, he tracked the bills paid for each month of the year. At the top of the ledger, he wrote his goals for the year and whether he accomplished them:

1992 - $10,000 IN BANK + CD'S (DID NOT ATTAIN GOALS)
1995 - 1) ALL CREDIT CARDS PAID OFF BY JUNE
1995 - YES
2) $25,000 IN BANK + CD'S - YES & NO
3) REDUCE # OF CREDIT CARDS AND USE - YES
4) GO TO NASHVILLE, MEMPHIS + ELVISLAND
(GRACELAND) - NO
1996 - PAY OFF DR. BARDASH
BLAZER – NEW OR BUY
MARGE & TOM'S MARRIAGE JULY 6, 1996
(A GREAT DAY)
RETIRE?

The goals after 1996 changed from the more mundane of paying bills to the more profound of staying alive:

1997 - NEW CAR FOR PEG - N.G. [No Good]
NEXT YEAR
LESS USE OF CREDIT CARDS - OK
SURVIVE - OK
1998 - NEW OR NEWER CAR FOR PEG - N.G. [No Good]
NEXT YEAR
LESS USE OF CREDIT CARDS - OK
SURVIVE - ALMOST

From 1999-2009, the goal for each year said, "SURVIVE." From 2010-2013, the last year he wrote in the ledger, his goal simply stated, "STAY HEALTHY."

After he was diagnosed with cancer, the doctor asked him to keep a log of his weight. Following orders, Mickey created a four-column ledger sheet that he wrote on daily in the smallest type a human can possibly write with a #2 mechanical pencil. A few years later, upon the advice of his doctor, he added his morning and evening weights and eventually recorded a quick memory or two of what happened that day.

Looking through the ledger pages, I found:

FRI   10/1/99 194 [pounds]

TUE   5/16/00 195/198

SUN   1/28/01 197/200 SUPER BOWL GO GIANTS N.G
        [No Good - Giants lost 34-7 to the Baltimore Ravens
        in Super Bowl XXXV]

FRI   2/13/04 181/193 44 WONDERFUL YEARS W/
        PEG G.B [God Bless] HER FOR
        EVERYTHING SUPPOSED TO MEET JOHN AND
        SANDY @ SHORTWAYS HOPE THE KIDS STOP
        BY GREAT NITE @ SHORTWAY'S WONDER-
        FUL NITE G.B. OUR FAM. CRAMMED 12LBS
        IN ONE DAY LOTS OF BEER - WOW G.B. PEG +
        THE FAM [Family]

WED   1/11/06 184/187 T.G. [Thank God] WE HAD A
        GIRL SHE'S THE GREATEST

FRI   1/27/06 /187 SAW SEAN'S PLAY - GREAT - G.B
        THE FAM. + PEG

Each struggle or challenge brought us closer together. The family love tightened and thickened. The fear of losing Mickey was unimaginable, and I was brought to the edge the few times he was sick. Each time from the hospital bed, he reassured me all would work out fine and I believed him. We said the vows of "in sickness and in health" once and lived up to them.

Chapter 25

Pilgrimage

In April 2008, we made a family pilgrimage to Ireland. Twenty of us somehow were able to get all the school calendars, sports schedules, and vacation time aligned. God must have played a hand in that. My only regret was that Mick could not accompany us but he needed to stay close to home due to his ailments.

We visited my brothers in London first. That was a wonderful time. It was the first time my children met some of their cousins. We met at a bar on a Sunday. There were only three or four local patrons in this small pub but within two hours, after sightseeing around the town, there were over fifty of us having a great *craic*, or party. The pints of beer and drinks of whiskey flowed like water that afternoon. My niece and her husband, Siobhan and Peter, on my brother Paddy's side, were previously champion Irish step dancers and put on a little show for us. Not to be outdone, there is a picture of my sons and my English nephews putting on their own show by posing without their shirts on. The afternoon was filled with fun, love, and many stories.

We continued our travels the next day by coach to Stonehenge, rode the ferry from Wales to Ireland, and went by coach again to Waterford, Blarney Castle, and Killarney. During one of our nights out, I told Jimmy and Pat about Mary. I had not planned on revealing the secret that they had another sister, but I was nostalgic being back home in Ireland and a few too many drinks may have broken down my inhibitions. They quietly took in this new information and told me they loved me.

Margaret knew about Mary already. During her sophomore year at college, I had a mother-daughter talk with her about relationships and shared that I had given up her sister thirty-three years earlier. We hugged and cried and our bond only grew stronger.

From Killarney we traveled north to the pinnacle of the trip - Roscrea. We visited the house I grew up in and walked the grounds. Jack was still living there and it was great to see him again. He was limping around with his artificial leg and still had to read lips to understand us. By now, Jack had installed some electricity in the house and even indoor plumbing. He put a toilet in the house too under the stairs that my brothers used as a bedroom. He then took us down the road to visit our parents' grave. I had not seen it yet. Jack took great care of it.

That evening, the Stapletons organized a great night out with family and friends. We enjoyed seeing many Irish relatives still living in Roscrea and from the surrounding area. The Stapletons rented out a local bar for just our party and hired a local band to play music. This *craic* was as wild as the first. By the end of the night, my sister, Nellie, who had moved back to Ireland years ago, and I were singing to the crowd at the microphone. Don't ask me what I sang, but we had a grand time.

The next day we drove to Dublin before flying home. I was glad my family was able to see Ireland and their relatives. Family is everything. As I flew over the Atlantic, I thought about Jack and my good-bye to him in the driveway. That was the last time I saw him.

Chapter 26

The Call

"Well hello, Nellie. How are you now?" I said as I picked up the phone. I looked forward to our monthly chats. The calendar on the wall was turned to September 2008. Instead of launching into our regular gossip and family news, Nellie said, "A nun from Sean Ross Abbey called me about you. Your Mary is looking for you."

I told Mickey about the phone call and then I told Margaret. I called Sister McManus in Ireland based on the information Nellie shared with me. I spoke with her briefly and gave her permission to share our phone number with Mary. She did ask me whether I had told Mickey about Mary. Because I listened to my mother's advice so many years ago, I was able to tell the sister that I had. Mickey and I then decided to bring the six of us together for a family meeting.

The next afternoon, we gathered in the living room, sat in our usual spots, and I told the children that Mary was looking for me. Michael only learned about Mary that day.

In the cramped living room, the TV was shut off and the family discussed the ramifications of the call. My children were very supportive but also nervous. They asked, "What does she want from us? What do we say to her?" We worried that Mary was mad about the

163

adoption and maybe wanted to vent on me about her life. While we all talked, Mickey was quiet. I knew this was not an easy conversation for him.

When Mickey did speak, he was very clear about his intentions. "Today, we start a new chapter in our lives," he said. "We look forward, not backward. We will move forward from this day on and Mary will be a part of us. We will only accept her. The case is closed." After the long talk, we agreed no one was going to break up our family and we should see what she had to say.

Pat approached Mick before he left the house. He asked, "Dad, are you okay with all of this? This is big, and we want to make sure you are alright."

Mickey responded in his quiet voice, "Thank you, Pat, for asking. I am more than fine with this. We have prayed for Mary our whole life together."

A few days later, Mickey answered the phone in the "funny room." We called it that because it was the small all-purpose mud room off the kitchen that housed all the extra stuff. When the two back room additions were put onto the house, we left the sheetrock up for a while before the paneling was nailed on top of it. Everyone who came to the house had a chance to write their name, saying, or drawing to be forever buried behind the wall. Mickey was a great artist and drew several cartoon figures and a heart with "Mick & Peg" written in it. The room led to the back porch and it had a countertop attached to the wall where Mickey did his official business like paying the bills, sorting the mail, and answering important phone calls. He was talking to someone and asking all kinds of questions.

All of a sudden, Mickey called, "Peg! Mary from Ireland is on the phone."

Oh, dear God.

Even after the family meeting, I was anything but prepared for the call. However, Mickey was. Unbeknownst to me, Mickey created a list of twenty questions when we first found out Mary was inquiring about me. Mickey asked them in rapid succession because he was being his usual thorough self and protective of me. We still did not know who Mary was or if she had any ulterior motives. So Mickey asked his questions he had written out ahead of time on a white lined pad of paper. Mary answered them one by one.

Mickey asked, "What is your name?"

"Maggie Boler. I am a teacher and I am fifty-three years old. I was born on April 24, 1955."

"Got it. Did you say, 'Bolder?'"

"No. Boler."

"B-O-L-L-E-R?"

"No, only one 'l.' My maiden name is Timmons." Mickey wrote "Timmins" with an "i" in his notes.

Mickey asked, "What kind of name is that?"

Mary said, "My husband is Polish and Danish."

"No Irish?"

"No. Just my side."

Mickey then asked several questions about her address and contact information so as to be able to stay in touch in the future.

"Are you married?"

"Yes, Tom and I have been happily married for twenty-nine years."

"Did you get an education?"

"Yes, I graduated from Illinois State University"

"That is why my wife gave you away, so you would have the opportunities she didn't have." He started explaining things to her.

Mickey continued, "Are you doing well?"

"Very well."

"How tall are you?"

"Five feet, seven inches."

"What are your children's names and ages?"

"I have two children – a boy and a girl. Meghan is twenty-four and Alex, short for Alexander Thomas, is twenty. They have both graduated from college. We also have two dogs named Shelby and Sammi – Golden Retrievers."

"Where did you grow up?"

"Illinois."

"When did you know you were adopted?"

"When I was eight years old. I was told by a kid in the neighborhood."

"Who gave you our names and info?"

"Sister Mary McManus was very helpful in us finding you." Sister Mary gave Mary my phone number after I gave her permission to share it.

"Do you have any brothers?" Mickey continued.

"Yes, my brother is thirteen years older."

"Are both your adoptive parents deceased?"

"Yes."

"White Sox or Cubs fan?"

"White Sox. Tom's father has season tickets to Soldier Field, so we see the Bears play all the time."

"Mick, shut up! I want to talk to her," I shouted from the kitchen table.

"Okay. I am going to get Peg on the phone. I don't want you to be mad at her," Mickey continued.

"No, I'm not mad. I can appreciate what she did for me," Mary responded.

Mother of God. A tidal wave of thoughts went through my mind. I was having difficulty breathing. My thoughts went back to Ireland.

I was thrilled Mary found me, but the pain became real again. The pain of the torment and teasing, giving Mary up, and leaving home for a foreign land. So much that was hidden and suppressed suddenly came to the surface.

It wasn't her fault. I gave her away to strange people so she wouldn't have to live like I did. I never thought of finding her because the adoption was supposed to be closed as they always were in those days.

"Peg," Mickey said to me. "Your daughter is on the phone."

As I nervously reached for the phone, Mickey said, "She's good. She's alright."

I did want to talk to her, but I didn't know what to say. I felt nervous, excited, and numb all at once. He told me not to be nervous and handed me the phone. I hesitantly said, "Hello?"

Mary started, "Mom? I want to thank you for giving me away. I know why you did it and that it was not an easy decision. I want you to know everything worked out and I am alright."

"Thank you, Mary." It was all I could do not to break down when I heard her words. I was so glad to hear them. I feared she hated me all these years. The Irish guilt came flooding back, and there's never anything nice when that happens.

I asked, "Do you have any children?"

"Yes. I have two, a girl and a boy." I got a little bit teary-eyed at this news. It was a moment when I realized my family had grown by two.

"That means I have thirteen grandchildren. You have three brothers and a sister."

"I always wanted a big family."

"Well, you've got one now."

"Where in the country are your children living?"

"They're all here. I live in Hawthorne, New Jersey. All my

kids and grandchildren live here in New Jersey."

"You all are so close. Do your kids know about me?"

"Yes, they do. I told them you were trying to contact me."

"I want you to know you did the right thing."

"I've been waiting fifty-two years to hear that. I really want to thank you for telling me that." My heart melted hearing Mary's words. "Mary, I'm sorry I gave you away but I wanted you to have a better life."

"It's okay. I am glad you did. It all worked out. I'd really like to meet you."

"I'd like to meet you too."

The conversation continued a little longer about our lives. At the end, I told her I was glad she found me and I hoped we'd get together.

I called my daughter Margaret right after to tell her the news. People who have known her since college call her Maggie. She had been a physical education and health teacher for eighteen years at Ramsey High School and married to Tom for eleven.

I said, "Mary goes by the name Maggie. She married a guy named Tom and she is a teacher."

Margaret screamed into the phone, "Mom! Are you kidding me? Maggie, Tom, a teacher! Just like me!"

"Oh, my God!" The coincidences just hit me.

I started to scream to my husband while Margaret was on the phone. "Mickey! Mickey! Maggie is a teacher married to Tom!"

Mary and I talked a couple more times on the phone in the following weeks. I remember Mary saying how grateful she was that I did give her away. When I asked Mickey how he felt, he said, "I'm happy she has an education. That was part of the reason you gave her away, so you have nothing to worry about." Mickey was very cool about everything.

My prayers were always the same. I prayed to God to help me get over my guilt, and He answered my prayers. After each conversation with Mary, I could feel the healing continue. I began to feel like a person who was more sure of herself. I was no longer stuck beating myself up over something I have no control over anymore. I told myself, *Enough already*. I cried so many nights after I gave Mary away and when I was by myself. Finally hearing Mary's voice and everything she had accomplished in her life shot through me to my core and started to heal me within. It was confirmed I did the right thing.

Chapter 27

Anticipation

January 22, 2009

Dear Peg (mom),

Well, what a ride we've been on! I am sitting here the night before I am to leave. So many thoughts are whirling in my head. So many questions to ask. But as I sit here I think about the miracle that has been handed to us. What are the chances that we would find each other? How very hard that must have been to give up your child. No one, including me, could ever know all the heartache. But so many factors invade our lives that steer our courses. Your selfless act of love gave me a life so filled with love and security. I owe you my life. I know after having my own children that what you did to give me a better life was the best gift a mother could give her child. I was blessed with a mom who committed her life to raising me with a firm foundation rooted in family. I wanted for nothing and my dad always believed we were related somehow.

This journey we are about to undertake is a gift from God. I truly believe my mom and dad are looking down and smiling because now I have an extended family to love and be loved by. I was raised in a very small family and yet there was a part of me that longed for more brothers or sisters. Now you have blessed me with both. My only regret is for all those years of worrying you must have endured. But to know I am about to meet you and Mick, and Michael, Patrick, James, and Maggie along with my beautiful nieces and nephews, is the most wonderful feeling.

Please know I have nothing but respect and admiration for what you did so many years ago! You did the right thing!! How hard that must have been to not know where I was and not be able to talk or watch me grow! But you are a woman of honor and high values. I am so excited to have you in my life. Thank you for entrusting me into the care of such great parents. When I lost my mom, a very big part of my heart went with her. You have filled that space in a special way that I don't think she would have minded. Not many children get a second chance to love a mother after losing one.

Thank you for wanting to make this connection and may we have many years together to join our families as one!

May the road rise up to meet you
May the wind be ever at your back
And until we meet again,
May God hold you in the palm of His Hand.

Love,
Mary (Maggie)

Chapter 28

United

Mary and I continued to talk on the phone and we mailed each other family photos. Wanting to finally meet each other, we thought it would be easiest for Mary to visit me in New Jersey. We settled on a date and she came out for Margaret's party. We figured it would be a great way to meet everyone. Mary felt she might as well get it over with and meet as many people as she could at once. In addition to the four newly found siblings, Mary gained a brother-in-law, three sisters-in-law, and eleven nieces and nephews.

Mary flew out to Newark Airport to stay for a weekend and celebrate her new sister's fortieth birthday. Her husband Tom was willing to accompany her but after talking it through with him, Mary knew she would be meeting many people and she did not want to overcomplicate things. She was not afraid to come alone. She caught a United flight on January 23, 2009, and landed at 9:20 P.M.

I was so nervous prior to Mary's arrival. I kept having thoughts, *What if she doesn't like me? What if she's mad at me for the rest of her life?*

Mickey, my children, their spouses, my granddaughter Erica, and I went to greet Mary at the airport. On the way down, Tom had warned us that not everyone is like an O'Hagan and we should be prepared in case Mary was a little reserved. It may take her a little while to absorb the whole moment and family since she was coming alone and there were many of us. We waited in nervous anticipation at the security gate for her to arrive.

We did not know what she looked like, but when she cleared the gate, I knew it was Mary. There's no way I could say that's not my kid. I'm looking at her face thinking, *Jesus Christ, Peg, that's me. She's just like me.* Mary was pulling her carry-on suitcase behind her in one hand and had her cellphone in front of her in the other recording the whole event.

Mickey, who was quiet and anxious, whispered in my ear, "She's just like you, Peg. It's okay."

As she walked closer, there was a building anxiety and then screams of excitement. When she was close enough, we embraced. It was unfathomable, as Mickey liked to say. I was overwhelmed with emotions for Mary and how my family was showing her love. I repeated in my head over and over, *God is not mad at me anymore.* I exhaled a deep breath I had held for fifty-two years. Whatever I did, I did the right thing for her, for me, for everybody else. All the guilt I held for these many years quickly began to vanish.

The way Mary accepted me was very important too because I didn't know if she liked me or not. It had been such a long time. She was so young when I gave her away. She was only a baby, for Lord's sake. I wondered what she turned out to be and if she was a happy person.

We hugged for a long time as tears came out of our eyes. When we were done, Mickey gave her the flowers he purchased for her and he too embraced her for a long time. It was very emotional for all of us. We took a group photo at the gate underneath the United sign not realizing at the time the irony of the airline name. Tom recorded the whole event with a handheld video recorder. When he saw Mary screaming, the hugs, and the cries, he realized his cautionary words were no longer necessary. He shrugged his shoulders at Margaret and said, "I guess she is an O'Hagan."

After the greetings, hugs, and kisses, Mary and I walked hand-in-hand out of the airport to the car. Looking at us from behind, my family could not get over how similar we looked. Jimmy said to Margaret, "There is no denying that Mary is her daughter." My children said the age-old question of nature vs. nurture was solved that day. There was no doubt that Mary was my biological daughter. Shortly thereafter, we arrived back at my house to celebrate this reunion. Coors Light and champagne were drunk as stories were exchanged. My children, including Mary, did a lot of the talking and Mary fit right in not missing a beat with sharing stories. It was boisterous sitting around the wooden kitchen table where we gathered for many previous family discussions, and everyone got along so well. It seemed as though Mary had been a part of our family all along. It was such a wonderful feeling seeing Mary in my kitchen for the first time. It was absolutely beautiful because I watched how *all* my children were accepting each other.

The bond was instantaneous and the love palpable. I was worried whether my children would accept her or resent her coming into our lives. My children were concerned about whether Mary would fit in with the family, whether the family dynamics would be affected, whether she would be angry, and whether she would even like us. But these feelings dissipated upon our first meeting at the airport. Mary was immediately accepted and as I watched all my children interact in the small cramped kitchen of my home, I saw how Michael, Jimmy, Pat, and Margaret loved her immediately.

My son Michael said to me, "Mommy, I knew there was something missing in your life for a long time."

175

I said, "What do you mean?"

"Every holiday you were sad."

"Really, Michael?"

"Yes. You were sad and now I know why. You were sad for your missing daughter."

"I was sad, but I didn't think it showed."

"It showed. Every holiday." I never thought others could see my sadness, but my son Michael obviously did.

Michael continued, "You look like there is a huge weight off your shoulders. You look ten years younger. You know, Mom, I always felt you emphasized the fact that I was your oldest child or first born when you introduced me to people. I never knew why. I hadn't thought much of it until now. I am not your oldest. I am your oldest with Dad."

"You're right, Michael. I did do that. I didn't realize it at the time, but I guess saying that helped me cope with the situation. It made me feel whole to recognize the family I had with Mickey and the life we built together."

The stories in my kitchen continued late into the evening until everybody left and Mary remained with Mickey and me. She slept over that weekend and we talked and caught up on fifty lost years.

The next evening we celebrated Margaret's fortieth birthday party at a bowling alley. When Mary and I entered the alley, my children were amazed to see us both wearing the same bright Kelly green fleece jacket with a large Irish Claddagh ring symbol and the wording "love, loyalty, and friendship" on the back. I chuckled. *My daughter and I were dressing alike. Unfathomable.*

Laughing, Margaret said to us, "Did you two go shopping together today?"

Mary, laughing too, replied, "No. I bought mine online a while ago. Mom had hers in the closet. We coincidently put them on today. We did not know the other owned this jacket. We love them."

Margaret said, "You could possibly be the only two people in the world who own them."

Margaret's birthday party was a wonderful night of bowling, pizza, and beer. There were close to eighty people in attendance and Mary's story quickly became the talk of the party. It was a little weird introducing Mary as my daughter or for my children to introduce her as their new sister, but everyone was very accepting of Mary and happy to meet her. You could see the quizzical look on people's faces when they heard that introduction. Mary and I were asked many questions and we happily repeated our story.

Coincidentally, over the years, Mary and I also were in bowling leagues. For me, I enjoyed socializing with a group of girls and getting some exercise. Mary and I did particularly well on the lanes that night. Noticing Mary had a few strikes in her frames, my seven-year-old granddaughter, Hagan, commented to her, "No wonder you're such a great bowler – *your last name is Boler.*" We had a good laugh.

Although we had ten lanes to ourselves, there was still some interaction with local townspeople at the bar inside the bowling alley. A patron at the bar saw Mary getting a lot of attention. He began to talk to her and asked some inappropriate questions. When Michael saw this interaction transpire, he approached the man and told him it was time to go. When the man questioned what he meant, Michael pointed to his brothers and all the other people in attendance and explained how it would be in his best interest to leave quietly through the side door. The man looked at Michael, saw that he was serious, and sheepishly went out the side door.

The last thing Mary wanted was to intrude in our lives and cause problems. She told Michael that he did not have to kick the man out, but a good friend of Margaret's interjected and simply said, "You're family now. Welcome to the family." The situation was resolved and the family grew by one. Once in the family, you enjoyed the love and protection of all.

The next morning, the family gathered at AB&G restaurant for brunch. The Outlaws, as the spouses of my children are affectionately referred to, and everyone present listened intently to what I had to say because I opened up about my past and revealed things that I had never spoken of before. Judy and Robyn, the wives of Jimmy and Michael respectively, asked many questions about the baby and my life when I gave up Mary. I found myself talking more and more about the story that I had suppressed for so long. But with many questions quickly coming at me, I was a little overwhelmed. I needed some quiet time to recall the past.

After we were all fed, toasts and cheers went around the tables and then Mary asked for the floor to make an announcement.

"I want to thank all of you for welcoming me into this family. You have been very gracious, warm, and loving. I truly appreciate it from the bottom of my heart, and it has been wonderful meeting you." As she was still speaking, several family members interjected our love for her and how we felt towards her.

Mary continued, "I love you too, and I just need to ask you one thing...I am in need of a kidney and would any of you wish to donate one to me?" The room erupted in laughter and Pat threw some bacon at her. There was a lot of tension the whole weekend with worry about who Mary was and what her true intentions were, but this crude joke helped break the ice. By this time, we knew she was a part of the family.

Chapter 29

Who's My Father?

After Mary returned home, we continued talking almost every day on the phone until we set up a digital camera on the computer to converse face-to-face via Skype. Because of the video stream, we were able to meet other family members at different times without leaving home. This was how I met her brother, Tim, for the first time at their family Thanksgiving gathering.

Mary and I discussed so many things. Typically we talked about our day, which then led into a story. Mary felt sorry for what I had to go through and what I felt I had to do.

I told her that is was not her fault that I had to go through that experience. It's something I had to live with. The only reason I gave her away was to have a good life and education. Since I wasn't able to continue my schooling I knew how important it was to have to be able to succeed in life. It was crucial for me that she had the chance I did not have.

During one of our conversations when she was visiting, Mary asked about her father.

"I would like to meet my father."

For a moment this bothered me. I had not thought about him

for a very long time.

I said, "I would too." Mary began laughing out loud. I corrected myself. "No. I don't want to."

Mary continued, "What was his name?"

I hesitated, but Mickey, sitting in his wobbly black armless chair hunched over the counter paying the bills, shouted his name from the funny room. I had not remembered telling Mickey this fact, but obviously I did at one point and he never forgot it.

After Mary and I laughed at this interruption, I followed up, "Mary, I got pregnant and it should never have happened, but you know what? It did. First of all, I don't think he knew I was pregnant. I really don't think you're going to accomplish anything trying to find him. He could be dead. I don't know. I will tell you, though, he was a nice person. He was several years older than me. We were together one afternoon. He didn't rape me. We were two feckin kids making asses of ourselves. I don't want you to think anything bad about him because I had you, his baby. He was a very nice young man."

I wasn't sure what was going through Mary's head, so I blurted it all out. I know I was curt and the information raw, but who has time to think this all through? "I'm very sorry, Mary, I didn't bring it up earlier, but I honestly feel he didn't know I was pregnant, so I didn't tell him. I only knew it myself when I was seven months along with you."

"Thank you so much for telling me, Mom." After we first established a connection, Mary began by writing and calling me "Peg" or "Peggy." This quickly faded. By this time in our relationship, Mary started feeling comfortable calling me "Mom."

Chapter 30

Mary's Hometown

Mary invited me out to Wheaton, Illinois, to meet her family and friends the summer after we met. Margaret and Pat joined me. I was so nervous. Flying gets me a little upset, but now I was going to meet strangers who love Mary. *What will they think of me – a mother who abandons her child?*

Mary and Tom threw a big party in their backyard with many people. Most of the night I was trying to hide, but everyone was very warm and engaging. The guests treated me like I was the Queen of England. Everywhere I sat, the guests sat around me like I was an exhibition at the zoo and asked me questions or told me stories. After maybe an hour or so, I said, "You do know I gave Mary away, right?"

Many kept telling me how brave and strong I was. I said, "I'm not that great a person. I don't feel as great as you think I am."

One responded, "What do you mean?"

I said, "I gave Mary away."

"Well she's the best thing that ever happened to Chicago. You didn't do anything wrong." They were so sweet to me. Pat kept close to me and a watchful eye. He was still protective and a little skeptical of others, but as he saw how genuine everyone was he eased up a little.

The next day when we were recovering from the party, I asked Mary, "Where are the pictures of your mom and dad?" I did not see any on the tables around the house.

"I put them away."

"You don't have to do that. They gave you the things I could not. Get their pictures. Next time I come out here, I want to see their pictures."

"How come you realized that?"

"They should be out. I'm the one that hatched you and gave you away. They raised you."

"You're right, Mom." Mary made us some tea and we carried our cups into the living room. I asked her to tell me about her parents, and as we sat on the couch we began to peel away the layers of so much we had missed together.

Mary began, "My parents were older when I was adopted. My father's name was Harry M. Timmons, Jr., and my mother was Dorothy. Her maiden name was Wyatt. They lived not too far from here in Glen Ellyn. We lived in a pretty middle-to-affluent area. Dad was a civil engineer and Mom was a stay-at-home mom. When they met, she was working at Marshall Field's as a timekeeper. But she never worked as far as I have known when I was with them."

"And your brother?"

"His name is Harry M. Timmons III. Before him, Mom had lost a daughter to a heart condition. The baby died two days after she was born. She had my brother naturally and then for some reason was told she was unable to conceive after that. When my parents were a little older, they proceeded to look into adoption."

"How much older is your brother than you?"

"Tim is thirteen years older than me. He is typically shy and quiet."

"Your parents decided they wanted another baby?"

"They did. I think they waited, tried and tried, and then realized, no, a baby is not coming, so as they grew older they knew they needed to adopt if they were going to have another baby. They were young enough to take care of the baby, yet not too old that the baby would wear them out."

"Did they tell you where you were born or anything?"

"No, they never told me until much later on. There was a lot of love in the house. It was almost like I was an only child because my brother was going to high school when I joined them. Growing up, I don't remember having too much of a relationship with my brother because of the age difference. When I was entering kindergarten, he was drafted into the Marines following in my father's footsteps.

"Unlike me, my parents were on the quiet side. I think I was closer with my dad. Mom was the disciplinarian and Dad was kind of a soft touch. I remember he'd say, 'Somehow we're related because I have people from Ireland.' *And then I'd wonder*, Why did he say that?

"My parents were married in 1941 and Dad was drafted into the Marines in 1944 for one year. Mom was a Protestant but converted to Catholicism in '45. My parents had a sincere appreciation for parochial schooling. They regularly attended Mass, and my dad was a member of the Knights of Columbus.

"Dad was a nice-appearing man with a ruddy complexion. He was easygoing, steady, and had a good sense of humor. He worked hard and enjoyed golf in his spare time. Mom was only 5'3", had a fair complexion, round face, and wore glasses. She was a pleasant, unaffected woman who was very much interested in her home and family. She was a sponsor of the local 4-H Club and a secretary of the DuPage County Home Bureau, which dealt with home economics. Dad had a brother and sister, but Mom was one of eight surviving children with several others dying during childbirth."

"Did you play any sports?"

"I was very athletic. Since we lived on a dead-end street, the kids in the neighborhood played on our block. I played softball, hard-ball, and football with the guys. Playing with these kids helped me develop my athletic skills because it was way before Title IX." Title IX was the 1972 federal civil rights law that protected women from discrimination in any education program including athletics. This amendment opened up the doors for women everywhere. "I never played organized sports at this stage of my life but was outside all the time playing with my friends. We never came inside."

"And when you were older, did you start playing organized sports?"

"Yeah, softball is a sport I really did play a lot. I played in eighth grade in the park on district-like softball teams. Basketball not so much. Never soccer or anything like that. I played fast-pitch softball and volleyball when I went to College of DuPage, or COD for short. It was a junior college. After two years, I then finished my degree at Illinois State University, where Meghan, my daughter, attended and played soccer."

"All of my children are athletic. I guess it runs in the family. How were your parents with you attending college away from home?"

"They were happy for me, but I could tell they were upset with me leaving. After my parents dropped me off, I sat on my bed. My first thought was, *I can have pizza at midnight.* It was the stupidest thing I thought, but I'm thinking, *Oh, my God. I have freedom I've never, ever experienced before.*"

"You said your parents never told you about the adoption. How did you find out then?"

"I still remember in second grade or so playing outside and one of the girls on the block said to me, 'Who cares? You're adopted. Those aren't really your parents anyway.' I remember running home screaming and crying to my parents. My mom told me to wait there and she stormed across the street. I don't know what happened over there, but she came back and then had to deal with it. She told me I was adopted. I don't really remember 'the talk' but she must have explained it really well because I don't remember being traumatized whatsoever. What's really kind of odd is that I found out her friends and neighbors had a shower for my mom before I arrived. They had a baby shower when they knew the adoption was final. So all the neighbors knew. Obviously, the girl's parents must have been talking in front of her one day and brought up that I was adopted."

"I am so sorry, Mary. Was it difficult for you?"

"I never felt like they were not my parents. I actually embraced it and wore it as a badge of honor. I told kids in school I was born in Ireland and was adopted. I remember a time when a teacher asked the class, 'Was anyone born in Illinois?' Hands went up. Then she asked, 'Was anyone born in another country?' My hand shot up right away. Then I was able to tell my story or as much as I knew. I never hid my adoption.

"I remember when we drove on vacations, the running joke my parents used to say was, 'Peggy is the only one in the family who's been on a plane.' Then they gave me little snippets of Ireland and the adopted thing but nothing big."

"You were blessed to be over here in America. You were given everything you needed. That's what I wanted for you." It was very bittersweet. "Mary, what were you called growing up? I see everyone here refers to you as Maggie."

"Growing up, the kids called me 'Peggy' or 'Dips.' My eighth grade softball team was named 'Dips' and somehow I acquired that nickname. It wasn't because I was dippy or anything, but I still had that name when I attended my junior college."

"They called me 'Margaret' in school, but my parents called me 'Peggy' or 'Peg,' which is very weird because they liked the name they gave me – 'Margaret Mary.' I think they called me that after the nuns. There seemed to be tons of Sister Margaret Marys at that time. But they never called me 'Margaret.' I don't know why they reversed the name you gave me, but I believe they flipped the Mary Margaret. Funny thing is I called my brother 'Timmy' even though he was named 'Harry' after Dad. I called him 'Timmy' as a nickname after our last name Timmons when I was young but then 'Tim' as I got older."

"You have so many names. I am surprised you're not confused. What was your relationship like with your parents?"

"They were very protective of me, extremely protective. I don't know whether it was because of the large age difference of how old I was to them, because I was a girl, or because I was adopted, but I didn't get to do anything my friends were able to go do. I think my parents did not know how to deal with me because my brother was very quiet and kept to himself. When he came home, he went up to his room and didn't really interact with others. We talked to each other, but we didn't have a relationship per se. I was kind of a jerk to him – a brat really.

"When I received my driver's license I didn't drive for a year. I distinctly remember I was sitting on the porch and Dad came out and said, 'Will you get us some hamburgers?' I asked, 'Who's going with me?' You know, that kind of thing. I could never be alone in the car, never could drive my friends. He said, 'No, you can go get them yourself.' I was shocked. It's the stupid things you get excited about. But I was never able to go away with friends in high school or spring break in college. I couldn't do anything. I never went to a party in high school. But I was allowed to babysit."

"You did that often?"

"I was super good at babysitting and loved kids. Not your 'A' student really and I now can't believe I became an English teacher because I didn't think it was a strength of mine, but I truly enjoyed working and playing with kids. That is what led me to become a teacher."

"I raised my brothers and sisters. I guess it's genetic." We both chuckled at the thought. I continued, "I loved reading and learning in school but never advanced past the eighth grade."

"Mom and Dad sent me to St. Petronille, a private Catholic school, which was a real big deal. It was a whole $80 a year back then. I went to St. Petronille within our town for eight years. It was a very strict Catholic school with Mass every day but no uniforms.

"I loved reading and hated math. Sister Marcian, my math teacher, was phenomenal, and she loved me. She understood me. She brought me down when I was out of control and she'd tell me, 'I see more in you than what you are giving us right now. I believe in you.' All the students loved her. I loved her."

"You were the class clown?"

"I guess so. It was mostly because of talking though. I was very social and acted like a comedian to take the attention *off* of me, but it backfired and brought more attention to me.

"When I was more serious and had to read, I always picked those *Nancy Drew* mystery books and I also enjoyed the *Hardy Boys*. But in parochial elementary and middle schools we had to read some classics like *Black Beauty* and *Heidi*. Those kinds of books. I loved them."

"Did you enjoy any other books as you aged that really stand out?"

"I hated the ones like *Silas Marner* or *Old Man and the Sea*. Blahh. I enjoyed *The Catcher in the Rye*, which I thought was really, really racy. I think everyone knew there was a swear word on page eight or something. I loved *To Kill a Mockingbird*, those kinds of things. But they really were classics. It was a very controlled reading list because of the culture at the Catholic schools. I personally did not read anything ever racy and whenever I saw a book that said 'shit' or something, I was like, *Oh, my God!*"

"Well I hope I don't offend you because I say 'shit' much of the time." We both laughed.

Mary continued, "We watched a lot of movies growing up. I loved the old movies because with my parents being older, I was exposed to those types of movies. I watched Charlie Chan every Saturday or Sunday whenever it was on. We had a black and white TV and, since there was no remote controller, I had to get up for my parents to turn the channel. I remember they watched *Secret Agent Man* with Patrick McGoohan. I'd get out of my seat every time and clap and dance to the theme song in front of my parents and then sit down. They loved me and gave me attention but not in a spoiled way.

"You know, we had an intercom in our house my father commissioned to be built, and it was in all the rooms. We had the house on Van Damin built by a builder and we had to wait in a rental before we moved in. Dad kind of moved up. He worked for Taylor Forge Pipe Works in Cicero. Then he started moving up the ladder with them. We moved from there to this house."

"When you went to high school, you went to a public school?"

"Yes. There was a threat, which is ironic, that Francis High School, where my kids went, was going to be closed my senior year. Mom said, 'I'm not going to have you thrown out after three years.' I was going to go there and follow my brother's path, but my parents said, 'I can't take the chance of it closing your senior year.' They sent me to Glenbard West and Dad said, 'Finally, we're putting my tax money to work.'"

"That's the public school in town?"

"Yes. I was scared out of my mind at first. I went in there looking for my Catholic school friends and it turned out to be the best thing to attend a public school. I became very involved in the school, which I loved. I went on field trips and sang at Wheaton College every year thanks to our choir director, Mr. Whitecotton. It was awesome."

"Growing up were there big family gatherings like we have now?"

"No. Even Christmas was quiet. The four of us had Christmas dinner, but it was more sedate. Very quiet. Nothing like I am exposed to now with my family and you guys. I remember Mom ran a bridge club, so every month we'd have four people over at night. I thought it was really cool because they made good food when that happened. I'd grab the food and watch TV in the family room. They said, 'Be sure you come in and say hello.' Then I came in, said hello, and left. I really was raised as an only child, I feel."

"How much was religion in your life besides school?"

"I went to Mass every day at school and on Sunday with my parents. We prayed before meals and I prayed each night before bed. When I was younger they prayed with me, but as I was older I said my prayers on my own. I would say we were a very religious family, yes."

"Mary, I was praying for you all the time."

"I brought the adoption up now and then, but Mom was uncomfortable with the subject so I didn't start to really think about it until high school and college. It came up again because I needed a birth certificate for driver's education, which I didn't have at the time. But I specifically remember a TV show we were watching one night. It was about a girl who was adopted and wanted to find her mom. She said, 'I want to find my mom. It's not that I don't love you, Mom.' My mom was squirming in her chair, getting upset. She goes, 'I'm so scared you will want to find your mom.' I said, 'Mom, I'm interested that there is a chance she's alive. But you're my mom and you always will be. I just wonder sometimes. That's all.' It kind of calmed her down and I realized then I just had to drop it."

"How did she tell you about how it all happened?"

"She said I was adopted through Catholic Charities and I was

189

brought over by some big Irishman they sponsored to bring me to America. On the cusp of the adoption, Mom had to write a special letter to the organization because they felt my parents were too old to adopt. She responded it was Mary or nothing, and that convinced them. The sponsor flew to Chicago and my parents met him at O'Hare Airport. Mom said I was screaming and she was worried I was scared, but the minute the sponsor gave me to her I stopped crying."

I shared, "I was never taught anything about the birds and the bees or what to do with a child in Ireland."

"Neither was I, Mom. My mom told me one time that I could get pregnant if I kissed a boy. That's what she told me. And the Catholic schools, ha! I learned about my period from a school movie called something like *Susie's Sister is Home*. That's the time of the school year when they separate the boys from the girls to teach them about what is going on with their bodies. I was so naïve."

"You think *you* were naïve!" I laughed. "How did Tom and you meet up?"

"Tom's best friend, Mike, and I worked together during the summer. Several of us from J.C. Penney went out after work one evening. Tom met up with Mike and saw me at the bar with my coworkers and asked about me. Mike introduced us. Tom was going to DePaul University in Chicago and this was the summer before I left for Illinois State University. He asked me out and we started dating. He came down to ISU to visit me once or twice a month because he was stuck at home commuting to school. We became serious really quickly. Our dads were not happy because the phone bills were awful.

"One time when he was staying with me, my parents arrived at my dorm for a surprise visit. They called me from the lobby and I didn't know what to do. They would have died if they knew he was in my room, so I quickly ran down to meet them and we went out to lunch, leaving Tom behind.

"After graduation, I could not get a teaching job, so I landed a job at Polaroid as a secretary. We were married in April of '78 and I was finally able to find a teaching position at a parochial school for $8,500 a year. I taught every subject including phys ed, art, and music. I taught there for six years until I was pregnant with Meghan. By then I was making $12,150. Tom worked at Carson's, PepsiCo, and then Household International, so I was able to stay home. We discussed it and I was lucky enough to be able to stay home for a good ten years.

"I started to worry more about the adoption thing while I was pregnant because the doctors and nurses kept asking questions about my medical background to which I did not have any answers. Then Tom and I wondered, *What if I'm a twin*?

"My dad passed away in 1989 and Mom passed away in '98. That is when I started thinking about it. Later on, my brother, Tim, found an envelope containing my legal papers along with my Irish passport. Inside the passport was a picture of me, and my name, Margaret Holland. I started going on the internet and doing research. I did have someone contact me from Florida claiming she was my mother, in a nursing home, and that 'she's a little low.' You know, the money thing. I responded saying I did not believe I was being told the truth and then kind of put it on the back burner. I knew it was a scam."

Our tea was finished and it was getting late in the afternoon. We started to get hungry. Plus there was a pile of dishes in the sink. We hugged and walked back to the kitchen together. We began preparing dinner and washing the dishes like I did with my mother so many years before. Only this time, it went quickly, as we only had to rinse them and place them in the dishwasher.

Chapter 31

Catching Up

After flying home, Mary and I slowed down using Skype but still talked on the phone. We developed a beautiful relationship, making up for all the years we missed with each other. I told her stories about my life growing up in Ireland, and she either stared at me on Skype or listened to me on the phone intently as the words of my childhood poured out.

After her initial visit to Hawthorne and my follow-up to Chicago, her family's first journey to New Jersey was for our annual Memorial Day party where they met my family, extended relatives, and friends – old and young. After that, Mary came out every couple months to surprise me. We were able to get alone time during these visits because she stayed with me in Margaret's old bedroom. These were special moments I cherished. I enjoyed our quiet time together. We continued our conversations and caught up on fifty years of untold stories.

The day after the Saturday night family get-togethers when Mary visited, Mary and I attended 8:30 A.M. Mass at St. Anthony Church. As we passed by the church to find parking on the street, I made the sign of the cross. Mary asked, "Why did you make the cross, Mom?" I chuckled, "I don't know why, but I always do when I pass this church. It's weird because I don't do it when I drive by any other church."

When Mass ended, we drove a few blocks to eat breakfast at either Andy's Corner or Triangle Diner, affectionately referred to as "Nadia's" by us after the first name of the proprietor. Nadia's was a quaint diner usually overly and tackily decorated with whatever season or holiday it was. The employees wore hats with the "Yummy Time" motto along the front. Nadia was always working and typically one of the first people you saw upon entering. After saying hello to several of the regular diners, Mary and I went to the back booth where we typically sat.

As soon as we sat down, coffee was served if it was breakfast time or a diet Coke with a lemon if it was lunchtime. No menus were needed. Nadia then shuffled up to our table and, since she knew our orders so well, basically confirmed what she thought we would order instead of taking our order.

In her Armenian accent, Nadia said to me, "Eggs overhard, sausage, and rye toast."

I said, "Sounds good, Honey. What do you have for soup today?"

"Chicken noodle."

Mary said, "I'll have that too." Nadia walked away with our orders.

Mary chuckled at the whole encounter. Customers leaned over and started conversations with us or talked to us as they left the diner. Mary commented, "Mom, you're like the mayor here."

"I don't know about that. I don't even know half these people or at least I don't remember their names." We both laughed.

With each visit, we both felt more comfortable with each other, and Mary began to probe a little further with her questioning. She asked about her father and whether there was violence when she was conceived. I reassured her it was nothing of that kind, but it was not a date either. I explained how I knew him and that I was innocent and naive back then.

"When did you know you were pregnant?" Mary inquired. I told her my stomach started hurting and we brought in the local doctor. I continued with the story, "The irony was I didn't even know anything about sex. My first feelings when I found out were anger, but then fear set in. I knew it was best for you to be given away, but I was afraid you hated me over the years. I wondered about you every day. Were you being hurt? Were you okay? Everything a mother worries about regarding a child. Being the 1950s and 1960s, I had a negative self-image, believing I must have been a whore or slut. The nuns made me feel horrible and I felt dumb. I didn't go far with my education and I had to work."

"Mom, you're not dumb. You were just not educated in sexual affairs," Mary objected.

Our conversation continued and I told Mary a little about her birth. "When I was in labor, the nuns would pop their heads in the door. Nastily, they would say, 'Haven't you had that baby yet?' and then close the door behind them. Then I continued with my labor – alone. I was meant to have you. We both could have died with you being breech and the lack of medical attention at the place."

Mary asked about the abbey and what life was like at the convent. Mary said, "My whole life I thought I was not with you and the nurses cared for my various needs."

I corrected her, "No, you were always with me. I was very protective of you. They wanted to take you, but I didn't trust anyone. Every time they opened the door, I told them they would only be able to take you over my dead body. I told them I was taking care of you and you were alright. They eventually left me alone."

"That must have been very horrible for you. Sounds like you

were a bit of a stinker, not quiet and meek, but a very strong woman, Mom."

"I didn't like my life there. They said my dad was not going to come for me. They tried to make me lose hope. The one thing I knew was I loved you. I was going to keep you as long as I could. Then when I had to give you up, I had a guilty feeling and a hole in my heart my whole life. A chunk was missing in my life."

Mary grabbed my hand. "I can feel how much you hated the nuns and the convent. I could not imagine. I always wanted to meet you, but I never had that same connection to you that you had with me as a mom. I did not have that bond with you since you gave me away at such a young age."

"I was angry, scared, anxious, and guilty."

"You shouldn't feel guilty, Mom."

"But I did. That is what we were taught. I always worried about you."

Nadia came back to our table, her arms full of plates of our food, and belted out, "It's Yummy Time." Our breakfast was served and we continued our conversation.

Mary asked, "What was it like to come to America?"

"Dad handed me a one-way ticket and said, 'You're not coming back, Peg.' That reality hit me hard as I boarded the plane." I told Mary about waiting alone in the airport for Mrs. Mulligan, how close I became with the children, and the incident when I stood up to Mr. Mulligan.

Mary listened intently. We finished breakfast and kept talking while drinking our coffees. "You know, Mary, I have not spoken of this story to many people and haven't thought about the details in a long time. It's a little fuzzy, but the feelings are perfectly clear."

I leaned in and said, "Mary, you're such a great singer. I loved hearing you sing in church. You didn't get that from me!"

"I sang in high school and now sing as a cantor in church. I enjoy it very much."

"My kids tease me that I can't sing and that I only sing half of the words and fill in the rest with sounds." Again we laughed.

"My parents said I sang myself to sleep in Gaelic every night after I arrived. I assumed it was from the nuns or maybe I picked up on the vespers while I was in the bassinet." Vespers are evening prayers said in many Christian religious institutions that usually begin with singing or chanting.

"No, my parents sang a lullaby to you every night. They were a big part of your life."

"Well, the songs stayed with me."

"It was hard bringing you home and getting to know you better. The song I sang as a lullaby for you and the love I felt for you was real. However, I was scared because in the back of my mind I worried I may have to give you away."

"Wait! We left together?" Mary stared at me shocked. I could see her putting pieces of the story together.

"Yes, but things were getting too bad for us back in the village."

"I wasn't left at the convent?"

"No. I never left you there."

"I always assumed you had me and then gave me away."

"No. I brought you home with me and we lived with my parents."

"Was I able to talk to you when we were separated?"

"Oh, yes you were calling me 'Mama.' You called your grand-parents 'Grandma' and 'Grandpa.' When you were going to the airport that morning, you knew something was up."

Mary said, "I can only imagine the feelings an eighteen-month-old would have had like, *Why are you giving me up to this person?*"

"I believe you were less than a year old when I gave you up. I told the people picking you up, 'Don't hurt her.' Then walked away."

"Mom, all the papers and letters I remember seeing say I was a year-and-a-half old when I was adopted."

"Really? I don't remember the dates exactly."

Mary was extremely curious how my father got us out of the convent given that leaving was a rare occurrence. I told her I did not know exactly how we got out of the abbey, but I believed some money was exchanged. I don't know where Daddy obtained the money, but I suspected the good-natured Spunners helped us out again with the situation. It may have even been some sort of bartering system between the Spunners and Daddy working off the loan.

Mary continued with her questions and I answered the best I could.

We paid the check and left the diner.

Most of the talks Mary and I had were about my early life in Ireland and filling Mary in on the background. After many more conversations, a few more years of reflection, and past memories coming to the forefront, more of the truth came to the surface. As I recollected my past, I realized not everything I said at first may have been accurate, but as more details emerged the fuller story came to light.

Chapter 32

The Truth

That was the story I told myself and very few others for over six-ty years. I learned much later in life that trauma can play tricks on the memory as a way to allow one to cope with loss. The mind finds a way to enable one to carry on when feeling all is lost. Getting pregnant at seventeen, delivering a baby by my-self, giving my daughter up for adoption, and leaving for a foreign country were all traumas I went through within a one-year window. In order to survive, my mind suppressed many details of the multiple traumatic events I experienced. My mind only wanted to look forward towards the future, not backwards towards the pain.

Sixty-three years after that fretful day of leaving Ireland, I stumbled upon a white plastic crate containing folders of old documents when cleaning out the bedroom closet. I found my old passport, some letters, and a few pictures. As riveted as I was with these findings, I began to notice these documents did not coincide exactly with the way I remembered things. The truth, it turned out, was much more painful. I began to do research about unwed mothers in Ireland and Sean Ross Abbey, and talked more openly with fam-ily members who shared their recollections. Slowly, memories of my last year in Ireland began to emerge out of a fog, and events and emotions I buried deep down inside seeped into the light.

After deciding Ireland was no longer the place to raise Mary, my parents and I had no idea what to do next or who to even speak with. We decided I should return to Sean Ross Abbey to seek advice. In order to give Mary away, one of the nuns there suggested I find a sponsor through an adoption agency in Roscrea. With all my trips to town over the years, I never knew there was a place to assist in the adoption process for girls who had babies. *I was not alone in my ordeal? How many other girls were there like me?*

The agency was a relatively new office. Adoptions were illegal in Ireland prior to 1953. Previously, to get around the law, passports were administered for babies who were "boarded out" to families around the world. The Catholic Church of Ireland was against adoptions for fear a Protestant family would adopt a Catholic baby. Parliament finally passed the Adoption Act of 1952 due to pressure from many voluntary organizations and the overcrowding of mother and baby homes. However, to pacify the Catholic Church, several clauses were included in the Act. There were two main clauses that affected me personally. First, a child could only be adopted by a family of the same faith; and second, it was illegal for children under seven to be adopted by families abroad unless the child was "illegitimate," in which case the child could be adopted if over the age of one. Mary fell into this latter category. By 1974, of the 5,252 babies born to unwed mothers at Sean Ross Abbey, the Sisters sent 438 to the United States for adoption. Mary was one of them.

Finding out the news it was possible for Mary to be adopted, I rode my bicycle to town to seek help. Exasperated and hopeful at the same time, I blurted to the man at the agency that I could not let my baby be harassed here anymore and needed to find a new home for her.

The gentleman behind the desk at the agency was terribly

kind. I wish I could remember his name. He gave me a soft smile and said, "We can help you get your baby adopted."

My whole goal for Mary in life was for her to do well and be whatever she wanted to be. Nothing was going to stop her. There were too many dead ends here in Ireland. I was bright and did well in school, but my brothers and I only went to the eighth grade before we had to work. I didn't resent anybody because of our plight; that was the way things were, but I wanted so much more for my Mary. I wanted her to have all the things my parents could not give me and I could not provide for her if we stayed here together.

Although my hands were trembling, I filled out the paperwork and could almost see Mary living a better life already. There was just one more thing I had to do.

Several weeks later, the gentleman told me to return to the agency to interview a couple and a representative of an American couple who were looking to adopt a baby girl. He thought I would be happy with the choices for Mary. Again, I returned to the agency alone. My parents could not bring themselves to sit by my side during these meetings for fear of crying too much. There were three people waiting to meet with me. I was so nervous. I kept wringing my hands until I thought they were raw. I didn't know what to say.

The first interview was with the young couple. We met in one of the rooms in the agency and had a nice conversation. They said everything they needed to say to get the baby of their dreams. They told me they had dreamed of a baby girl and explained how much they wanted a family for themselves. They also said I'd be making a mistake if I didn't go with them. That made me nervous.

Next, I met with a representative of an older couple with the last name of Timmons. I don't know what it was about George Ramelow, as I later found out was the representative's name, but I liked him better based upon what he was telling me. Mr. Ramelow told me how warm, gentle, and kind the Timmonses were. I liked the thought of them immediately. I decided Mary would go to the Timmons family and said goodbye to the young couple.

Although I did not know this during the interview, the Timmons couple were planning on doubling the size of their four-room house to two stories to accommodate the addition of their adopted child. They were anxious that the small size of their original home could hold up their adoption and were willing to move the start date of the addition earlier if the Irish authorities deemed it necessary.

The Timmonses requested to adopt a little Irish girl under three or four years of age. They would be very happy to take two children or twins if they were available. They would also be happy to take two children if they were a boy and girl; however, if it was a question of only taking one child, they would definitely like it to be a girl under three or four and preferably as young as possible.

The child welfare agency background check on them revealed they were a stable Catholic couple who maintained a happy and congenial home. They appeared to have done a good job raising their own son and sincerely desired to have a daughter. They would have applied earlier, but they always anticipated having more children of their own since they had one early in their marriage. While there would be quite an age difference between their son and adopted daughter, a child placed in the Timmons' home would receive good care, much affection, and probably better than average advantages. On November 23, 1956, the Catholic Home Bureau fully approved the placement of an Irish child for the purpose of adoption in the home of Mr. and Mrs. Timmons.

Within the week, paperwork completed, Mary and I drove one last time together. A relative drove us and we sat in the back seat. The land that brought her into the world and united us was now the same place that separated us. My arms were shaking as Mary and I exited the car and walked to the front door. We rang the bell, waited for the door to open, and looked into each other's eyes. Her beautiful hazel eyes looked up to me. The door of Sean Ross Abbey opened, and we were greeted by a nun.

"Peggy, so glad to see you...and Mary you look grand," the nun said to us on the steps of the doorway.

"Here you go," I said. "Make sure she has an education if it's possible."

The nun responded, "Yes, it's possible."

I pleaded, "Please don't hurt her. Please don't hurt her in any way."

"We won't. We will love her very much. Thank you, Peggy. I wish you the best."

"I wish you the best, too. Please take care of this little girl for me. Please."

"We will."

I bent down, took a deep breath, hugged Mary, and said, "I love you, Mary, very much. Now you have to go with this nun. I love you...I love you."

"Mama," Mary said in her soft angelic voice. I kissed her on the cheek. I almost left a mark I kissed her so hard.

I stood still for a moment, almost as if I was making a mistake. I knew I wasn't, but I had to force myself to think about this one last time before it was over and I would never see my baby again. I looked down at Mary and she was smiling. I swear, she was giving me permission to let her go.

The tears started to well up and I knew I could not hold it together any longer. I kissed her once again, turned, and did not look back. I walked quickly to the car so I wouldn't change my mind. I heard the front door to the abbey close behind me.

I was left alone with my thoughts on the rainy drive back

home. The tears in my eyes flowed as freely as the water from the sky. I cried with mixed emotions of joy for Mary and sadness for me. In my heart I knew I did the right thing, but giving up Mary was the hardest decision of my life.

When I returned home, my parents were still at the kitchen table where I left them. My parents were so upset they could not accompany me and I left them crying in the kitchen. They cried more over me giving up my baby than me being an unwed mother. They felt they had failed us since we couldn't care for Mary. I went upstairs to my room and cried myself to sleep. The next morning, I began packing my belongings. They fit in one suitcase.

The second thing I did after deciding to give Mary up for adoption came in the mail. I looked at my passport, which was issued by the Passport Office on March 14. I recently received it from Dublin after applying for it a few months back after the first adoption agency visit. The pain had become too great. My fear for Mary and the life she would live was too heavy to continue to live here in a place that once brought so much joy but now only brought sorrow.

Christmas was approaching and Mary was about eight months old. She was the most precious gift I had. I had never received a gift at Christmas but the season was about giving and now I could give others a gift and give Mary the gift of a better life. I gave Mary away believing God would take care of her.

Four months later, I rode my bicycle up the road to the monastery and said goodbye to Jim and Paddy. They were trimming the hedges. I gave them the ten remaining fags, Irish for cigarettes, I had in my possession. We made some small talk and then I gave them a big hug. I hopped on my bicycle to return home and I saw them each light up a fag.

As the fog of the trauma slowly dissipated, I remembered that I returned to the abbey for advice, that I only spoke with a representative of the Timmons family and not them directly, and that I gave Mary over to the nuns, who I previously swore would never take my baby from me, for the adoption process and not the Timmons at the airport. Remembering the details of adoption and giving Mary away were too painful to live with so I suppressed them until now. My mind remembered these details differently over the years to cope with the trauma caused by the events.

When looking at the documents in the file, I also realized the timing of it all. The dates on the paperwork brought me back to when the ordeal began. I had never thought of the significance of the exact dates when I gave Mary away and when I left for America.

The American Embassy in Dublin stamped my immigrant visa on April 24 and the U.S. Department of Justice admitted me into New York, New York on April 26, 1956, two days after Mary's first birthday.

Chapter 33

Magna Carta

O'Hagan and Gorman Families

Do not read until X-mas Eve when you are all together

December 25, 2010

Dear Family,

I don't know who was elected to read this but here goes. A very Merry Christmas to all of you and I can't wait to see you Wednesday. Enclosed you will find some dorky gifts from me to you! I hope you like them and think of us when you use them and say, "Wow is she a dork!" On a more serious note, whatever you may think about giving me...take it back!! You have already given me a gift to last my whole life. When we found each other, my life was complete. Every day I am in awe of how your arms opened and swooped me into your life. I know the credit for your unconditional love started with the two beautiful people you call mom and dad. What role models you had to grow up around! You should feel very blessed. I am blessed too for the sacrifice mom made to give me my beautiful life with my family here!

I don't know about you, but I'll find myself just thinking about how all this happened and just start smiling for no apparent reason. Not many people can say that. I want to take this moment to thank all of you for accepting my family and me. I will always remember the first time I came out there and we were at Sunday brunch. Beth Ann leaned over to me and said, "You know, Mary, it's like you have always been here but you have just been gone a long time!" That said it all for me, and I have grown to admire Beth Ann's strength and compassion for others as I have grown to love her.

Jim and Judy, you have given me three beautiful nieces who are not only physically beautiful, but the beauty that radiates from within each of them is quite an awesome quality. You two must be so very proud.

Michael and Robyn, Jules and Michael are two of the most kind and loving children. The love and caring Michael shows at such a young age is truly a reflection of the two of you! Jules is a beautiful young lady who has a depth of character hard to find in many teenagers. Thank you for sharing them with me.

Patrick and Beth Ann, how do you manage not to bust open with pride over those three children you blessed the world with? The spark of fire in Erin's eyes, the competitive drive of Patrick's spirit, and Jo Joe's sense of humor yet sense of compassion. Wow!

Margaret and Tom, the blessings you have brought to this family in the shape of Sean, Hagan, and Shea are countless. When I walk in the room, their energy and over-the-top love for their family shines through their beautiful faces.

Then there are the infamous outlaws. What can I say to four beautiful people that welcomed another loud relative into the family? I have only known you a little over 2 ½ years, but when I see you with my siblings, the love reflected in all you do for them and your children is amazing. You handle so much and juggle so many balls, and yet that is the reason Pat, Michael, Jim, and Margaret love you so much. Thanks for being such awesome spouses.

Now, to my siblings. Well if I could have placed an order with God, I couldn't have been more satisfied. To watch you interact with each other and listen to all your stories about growing up together I found myself envious yet thankful you had each other. My whole life I wanted a sister to hang with and share secrets with. And when I met you, Margaret, I felt you already knew all those secrets so we've already caught up. Took some time getting used to the Jersey circle of protection, but I am getting better. I am so proud of all my brothers and sister. You have become such wonderful men, husbands, and fathers, and Maggie, your compassion and love for your family is unmatched.

The best for last, Mom and Mick. I first found out that Mom had been honest with you from the start, and your response was, "Well Peg, that is just someone we will need to pray for." I knew I had met a man of integrity and faith in his love for mom and his family. Mick, you are truly one of the most remarkable people I have ever met! I thank you for loving mom when she needed it the most! I thank you for accepting me into your life when most men would not. And I thank you for giving me my dream family, because it is because of you and mom's hard work, love, discipline, and moral character that your children have passed on your passion for living and all that goes with it! You are (as Patrick said) the definition of what a real man is.

And what can I say to you, mom? You gave me life and then unselfishly gave me a life. I always want you to know that your decision shaped all our lives, and the circle of life led me back to you! I truly believe my parents are watching over me and are happy I have found you and have been given a second wonderful woman in my life to call mom.

This letter comes with a full heart, loving thoughts and gratitude beyond words to all of you for accepting me, loving me, and giving me a family to be proud of. I want you to know I love you and miss you every minute we are apart!

Merry Christmas and here is to a life together made up of dancing, laughing, and loving.

Family...First and Last!

Love,

Mary

P.S. I know I'm a dork, <u>but deal with it!</u>

Do Not Open till XMAS Eve

Magna Carta #2

X-Mas 2011

My Dearest Family,

As I sit here writing my second Magna Carta to you during this holiday season, I reflect on all the miraculous things you have brought to my life. (I can't think of any!) HAHA. Here we sit as our fourth year of miracles is about to begin. I can see you all sitting together during what my brother said were "the five best hours of the year" and picture in my mind all your faces sparkling with the anticipation of what this holiday will bring. I already know what you have brought me: love, respect, acceptance, loyalty, and an overpowering sense of commitment to family. You each have shared a part of yourself with me that is immeasurable. The gift of your presence at Meghan's wedding was astounding. Although you may think it was just what family does, to some people who live by us and we have known a long time other factors weighed in as more important. As my life goes on, my circle of trust is becoming much smaller. But I am a better person for it.

Each of you has made me so proud this past year with your love for each other and your willingness to go above and beyond for family and Friends…

Mom & Mick:

Mick, I believe my dad sent you to me to take care of me when he couldn't be here. He was a gentle man. Strong in his faith, tenacious when it came to protecting his family, and in love with his wife all their married life. (sound familiar?) When other men would have had great difficulty with this whole situation, you embraced it and showed your love for Peg in a very concrete way. Thank you for accepting me and giving me this beautiful family. They are the reason you are here, and I know you are their hero!! I only ask myself what I have done all these years without them and you. I love you!

Mom: I am going to try to thank you without losing it. I know it was hard to let go so many years ago, but I hope you are at peace about your decision and know that right before your eyes I have grown into as big an idiot as you would have wished for. Nurture vs. nature has been blown out of the water. Thank you for my brothers, my sister, my family. The strength of family you have instilled in all of them is quite an inspiration. I love you and I missed you all those years in my heart. Ya did good, lady!

Now I am through, and I do not want any shit from anyone

211

one! I shall see you soon and I hope you enjoy the picture and NO gifts. You are present enough. Much love and awe!!

Love,

Mary

Chapter 34

Searching

Mary visited whenever she could. We still talked on the phone often and kept each other abreast of what was going on in each other's lives. Each Christmas, she wrote a long letter summarizing the year and expressing her love for each individual gathered in my basement. Either Michael or Margaret read what Mary wrote during the middle of the annual Christmas Eve celebration in our basement. The room was respectfully quiet except for the outbursts of comments, roasts, or sound effects that related to whatever was just read. The letters were beautiful, but because of their length, they were nicknamed "The Magna Carta." When we were apart, Mary also sent cards that were filled with pictures and uplifting words of love inside:

Dear Mom & Mick,

I have enclosed some pictures for you from our trip. I found you later in my life and am trying to make up for all the earlier pictures you weren't part of. So, if I start becoming a pain in the _ _ _ by sending too many, let me know! I am just a card and "thinking of you" kind of gal! Since I can't see you as much as I would like, sending small reminders will help me seem closer! I am weird I know, but you're stuck with me!

XOXOXO   Love Mary & Tom, Meghan & Alex

Besides the diners, we often frequented Shortway's Barn. Dating back to the 1920s, this old barn stabled animals, provided a safe haven for customers during Prohibition, and has fed truckers coming off Route 208 and families from miles around. It has an old rustic look and many locals frequent the place, including the O'Hagans. Shortway's burgers are excellent.

Mary and I liked to go there on a Saturday or Sunday afternoon to have some quiet time together. We sat at the corner of the bar, talked, and had a few drinks. Mary had a draft of Miller Lite and I sipped on a Blue Moon bottle.

It was my turn to ask many of the questions now. I turned to Mary, "What prompted you to look for me in the first place?"

Mary told me of her adventure. "When I was younger, there was a moment I started asking questions and that kind of stuff. My mom was kind of funky about the whole adoption thing. I think she was worried about what I might find out. So I left the topic alone.

"After they passed, I began searching for you on the internet. I started with the ancestry sites and connected with some people. One woman from Florida said she was my mom. She emailed me saying she was in a nursing home and she had lived in Roscrea. Although encouraged at first, we eventually stopped talking. Another said she was my mother and I wrote to her but never heard back. I had not been searching too extensively at the time. It was relatively easy and lots of information came in, but the trouble was trying to weed through the information to determine what was real and legitimate.

"When my brother Tim and I were cleaning out our mother's

house, he handed me a folder with my father's handwriting on it. I went into another room with the folder, looked at it quickly, and yelled, 'Holy crap! Tim, this is my stuff from Ireland. This folder contains my passport, baptismal certificate, adoption papers, and so much more.' I showed them to my Tom and he said, 'We have to go to Ireland. We've got to go.' We bought tickets for Ireland that July 2008. Ironically, you had just traveled there in April.

"Prior to leaving for Ireland, I was warned by women on the internet that Sister Sheehan was a difficult roadblock to get around when trying to access the abbey's adoption files. She blocked many of the adoptees' pursuits to find their mothers. From some of the stories that were shared, I was tentative that I'd get anything from the nuns. Tom began planning out our trip to fill in the missing pieces. We began our trip in Cork. Cork was where the adopted children's files were sent from Sean Ross Abbey. We set up an appointment to meet with the nuns.

"When we arrived, I met this little Sister Mary in the parking lot of a convent in Cork. We walked up to this 5'2" nun and she happily greeted us. I questioned her saying that I've heard that Sister Sheehan usually handles this kind of stuff. She responded in her drawn out Irish accent that Sister Sheehan was on sabbatical that week. I told her that I heard some people who had been here had a tough time getting information for adoptees. Sister Mary smiled and said she would try to help me. In my mind I thought, *Sister Sheehan wasn't there? Are you kidding? Is this the luck of the Irish or Divine Providence?* After that brief encounter, Sister Mary was very accommodating and helpful with finding my files from Sean Ross Abbey. I brought all the information I had with me to Ireland. I had a lot more stuff than some adoptees to take to the convent to help with the search.

"After we gathered all the information they had on file about me, Sister Mary said she'd get a hold of us if she found something. We then traveled up to Roscrea and went to Sean Ross Abbey to walk the grounds."

"What were your impressions of the place?" I asked.

"We came down a winding road and went under the gate. It was very, very sterile-looking to me at first. It was used as a special education facility for special needs kids now. We walked the grounds and saw the cemeteries of the children who died, the moms buried, a very rudimentary cemetery, very old tombstones, and little crosses. I was aghast at that site.

"Nobody came up to us while we were there so I went up to the front door. Alex, Meghan, and Tom stayed back a little ways. I knocked on the door but no one answered. I entered the unlocked door and said to the first nun I saw in the hallway, 'Hello. My name is Mary. I was born here and I'm coming here to maybe get some information about my adoption.' Immediately, the nun yelled into another room, 'Sister, one of our babies came back.' I thought that was so kind and this may not be as bad as I thought. They brought us in, sat us in a room where they had all their photos of the place, babies, and children in photo albums. We sat and looked through them.

"I told them a little bit of my story. They were not overly excited, but they were very welcoming. They showed me the rooms of the abbey, showed me where the babies played during the day, and then brought me to the old nursery.

"I inquired whether you were still alive. I explained how I had been to Cork and acquired some information. But the nun just wished me luck in my search. I asked if I could walk the grounds and look around some more. We walked around a little while longer, Tom took a picture of me in front of the sign, which I had sent to you guys, we went to lunch downtown, and then moved on.

"On our last day of the vacation in Dublin, Sister Mary called. She was hoping to reunite you and me in Ireland if she found you. We all believed you were still living in Ireland. She had not located you but said she would keep looking if I wanted her to continue the search. There would be no money involved at all. I responded that I would love it if she could find family members or something."

I asked Mary, "How did you find me, Dear?"

"A few months later at 6:30 one morning, Sister Mary called from Ireland and asked me if I was sitting down. She said that she had contacted you and that you lived on the East Coast in New Jersey. She said she asked you whether you knew why she was calling and you said, 'My Mary is looking for me?' After your conversation, you gave Sister Mary permission to give me your phone number.

"Even though I had been searching for you all this time, I didn't know what to do with this new information. I ran upstairs, jumped on Tom, who was still in bed, and told him the news. Then I went to school. I remember almost running down the primary wing of the school telling everyone I worked with that the nun called me and I found my mother.

"My colleagues at work and friends knew this good news would come, but they didn't think it was going to be this fast. I told them I was going to call you that night. I thought about you all day, and then that night at 8:00 P.M., Chicago time, I told Tom that I am calling you now.

"I dialed the number and Mick answered. At that moment, I realized Sister Mary never told me his last name, so I stuttered sounding like a real idiot and finally said, 'Mick, I'm sorry. Sister Mary called me after talking to you guys and you had given permission for me to call. She never told me your last name. I think I'm your wife's daughter, Mary.'

"He yelled, 'Peg, she's on the phone!' Then he proceeded with his twenty questions. I knew he was asking them out of love and protection for you. I heard you get on the extension line and could tell you were listening. Then, after many of his questions were answered, you piped in and told him to shut up and get off the phone. Although he stopped talking, I knew he definitely stayed on the line listening."

"I remember. That's pretty much how it went. I was so nervous hearing your voice." It was time for another drink. We ordered another round from Tracy and placed our late lunch or early dinner, depending on how you looked at it, order. When we were in our corner at the bar, time seemed to go slowly or maybe even stopped. There was music in the background and sports on every TV in the establishment, but we could not hear the music and we could not see the games. We were caught up in each other's stories and our own little world.

Mary continued with her recounting of the first time we spoke. "I remember you tentatively said hello and I responded telling you that we received a lot of good news today, I think I'm your daughter Mary, and how Sister Mary called me that morning. I thought it was kind of weird that the nun's name was Mary too. We have Marys all over the place. I didn't want to bother you or for you to think I was invading into the life you've made, but I felt it was important to reach out. I wanted you to know that I was fine and that you did the right thing. I have a beautiful family because you sent me away safely. Over the years, looking at my two children, your grandchildren, made me realize how truly difficult it must have been to give up a baby at the convent.

"When I first spoke to Mick, my heart was not thumping like crazy. I was calm and in 'game mode.' I totally understood where he was coming from with all the questions. I knew going in that the family was probably thinking, *What does she want? Is she looking for money?* Over the phone, I could feel Mick's concern for you. My initial feeling from Mick was, *Why are you now coming out to find my wife and my family?* And from you, Mom, I thought you were feeling, *Oh, my gosh. It's my daughter I've worried about for fifty-two years.*

218

You said nothing harsh to me and I bet you probably thought I was going to yell at you. Mick was there, as he always was, to protect you."

By this time our cheeseburger and fries platters were served. I started eating my medium-cooked cheeseburger with raw onions and Mary picked at her fries.

Mary continued, "After we talked, there were a series of emails exchanged because I wanted to see what you looked like. Pat was the first to send me some family photos and pictures of your last trip to Ireland. I sent pictures in return of my family and me and asked if there was any resemblance."

"When we received them, Margaret noticed right away how much there was a similarity between us. She said our hands were exactly the same. That was just the first of many similarities we noticed."

"On the plane ride out, I kept saying to myself, *Oh boy, oh boy.* I was sitting on the plane, looking around at people and I wanted to burst out and tell everyone where I was going and why.

"When I disembarked from the plane and came out of the long hallway gate, I saw all of you standing there. I was overwhelmed. Then I saw you standing there. At that moment, I was wondering more about what you were thinking because you held the secret since you had me. I couldn't believe I found my mom. I had a life up to that point and, as I was looking at you, I was thinking that if I were in your shoes and I was staring at my daughter who I hadn't seen for fifty-two years, I would only be able to say, 'Oh, my God.' I thought more about what you were thinking at that moment. Then we hugged. It was unbelievable."

"Mickey said it was 'unfathomable.' He loved using that word."

I grabbed Mary's hand and said, "I am so sorry for everything. I am sorry I gave you away. I love you very much. I enjoy these conversations." A few tears came to my eyes.

Mary, who started to cry too, said, "I love you, too, Mom. I cherish these moments. I am glad you gave me up for adoption."

She continued, "Many times it is too noisy and crazy with so many people around. I am glad we have finally had an opportunity to dive a little deeper into the details. There are so many questions to ask and stories to catch up on."

We stayed a little while longer. Mary asked about the convent. I told her some of the stories and we tried to fill in the gaps in each other's stories. I asked her about her children. She filled me in on their lives. As we shared our stories, I started to remember more. Each time felt like more weight came off of me. I started feeling a little more comfortable telling the story and each time Mary and I met, we felt more comfortable asking the deeper questions.

Chapter 35

Enough

My youngest granddaughter, Shea, went to her First Reconciliation at Our Lady of Mount Carmel in preparation for Communion. I accompanied her since Margaret and Tom were not available that day. It turned out to be the most invigorating and satisfying experience in my life. As we stood in line waiting for the priest to become available, Shea asked me if I was planning to go to Confession. I told her I had no intention.

My eight-year-old granddaughter with an angelic face said to me, "Mum-Mum, you have to talk to him. You will feel better." She did not know that anything in particular was on my mind.

I quickly responded, "Shea, *you* have to talk to the priest, not me." *I had not been to Confession since before Mary was born.*

After Shea confessed to the priest and emerged from the small confessional stall, she looked at me and said, "Mum-Mum, you have to tell the priest what's bothering you. You need to talk to the priest, Mum-Mum." I will never forget that little face speaking to me. Either because of that eight-year-old look or a force greater than me, I went into the confessional stall and sat face-to-face with the priest. I had left the door of the stall open a little.

"Well, Father, I'm just not myself. I'm very guilty about a lot of things and I have not gone to Confession in a long, long time." I can see Shea waving to me. *Just let her be.*

"Okay, tell me about it. Why are you feeling guilty?"

Well, I blurted everything out. The priest kept nodding his head and affirming what I said. I didn't stop until everything was off my chest. That was all I needed. I confessed. I confessed it all to him. I had not been to Confession since before I left Ireland over fifty years earlier. Although I attended Mass regularly, I was petrified to go to Confession because of what I had done.

The priest said, "I really don't know what you're upset about or why you feel you did anything wrong."

"Well, in Ireland, you're not highly thought of if you have a child out of wedlock, and you were called all sorts of names."

"You have nothing to confess."

"I had a baby and I gave her away. I have never told a priest what had happened to me."

"Get over yourself with the Irish guilt."

"Is that what this is?"

He grabbed my hand and said, "Yes, that's what that is. You gave your baby away. She was in a better place and she's happy. I'm not even going to give you a penance because I believe you may have suffered enough all these years. Go on with your life."

The priest made it so easy. I said to myself, *I should have gone to Confession sooner.* But it would not have been easier for me if I had.

I said the Act of Contrition and before I left, the priest chuckled and said to me, "Do you see the little face outside the confessional? She probably told you to come in today."

Shea had been watching me through the open door of the confessional stall the whole time. Her face never moved and she kept watching me, making sure I did not get too upset.

"She did. That's my granddaughter."

He blessed me and sent me on my way. God works in mysterious ways, and this time he used my granddaughter to move me one step closer in my healing process. When I came out of the confessional, Shea grabbed my hand and said, "You feel better now, don't you, Mum-Mum?" After the confession, it was like somebody removed a rock out of my heart and threw it away.

Chapter 36

The Back Deck

The back deck could be accessed from walking up the long narrow driveway or from the house through the funny room. It was a place to gather throughout the seasons. It was a small wooden deck Mickey built many years ago. It could comfortably seat six people, but we typically had many more squeezed in tight. When too many gathered, it was only two steps down to the patio to hold the extra guests in the small backyard.

Mary and I continued to see each other several times a year. I had been out to her house five times both by plane and car. We continued to get to know each other and share in each other's lives. During the evening, it was quite nice to sit outside on the deck and enjoy the cool night air.

Mary began, "You know, Mom, we were so excited I found you. We couldn't believe it. Tom and the kids were always supportive of me whenever I spoke of trying to find you. I think I would have looked for you earlier, but I wanted to be respectful to Dorothy, my mom."

"I understand, Honey. I am glad you did find me."

"There was just that thing in my mind about Mom. I felt I

needed to be respectful to her, but when she died I felt it was finally okay to search for you. Tim was very protective of the family and me. When I told him I wanted to find you, he said, 'Why do you want to find her? You have a mom.' He was not thinking about the biological part of this whole scenario."

When we sat out back, Mick typically joined us. Despite his condition, he still sat outside to smoke. Although Margaret and the boys were very frustrated by this fact, they reluctantly acquiesced to this one vice since they realized he could no longer eat, drink, or do most things that brought him pleasure. What I would have given to allow him to eat a full meal of steak and potatoes with gravy. He had a three-pronged fork with a weathered wooden handle that he ate every meal with all the years we were together. When finished, he had a peculiar habit of asking permission to lick his plate, then held the plate parallel to his face and licked it clean by rotating it clockwise until it was spotless. He then sat erect in his kitchen chair that nobody else dared to use, with his feet flat on the floor, gently pounded his chest with his right hand, and let out a belch that could be heard throughout the house. He always acted surprised by the intensity of the belch and then excused himself. Margaret copied his belching habit but not licking the plate. But those days were gone and he was living on a liquid diet through a feeding tube in his stomach. Smoking was his one remaining pleasure. He slowly dragged on his Camel cigarette and let the ashes fall onto the deck, which he then flicked away with an old slightly burned fly swatter. Mary and I had a few beers and talked. Mickey listened.

Mary shared, "Growing up, I was a little different than everyone else in the family. I enjoyed sports and was loud, outgoing, and full of energy. I was kind of the black sheep of the family. But when I met all of you, I realized how much biology does play a role in family genetics. It started to make sense of who I was and how easily I fit in with all of you.

"Each time I've visited, I have tried to get to know everyone a little more intimately. At first, I didn't know what you were thinking about me. Maybe it was like, *Okay, we've met her once and now we can see her once a year. That would be nice.* That is when I started to write the Christmas letters. I didn't think we would be seeing each other as much. I came out a few more times and I cannot believe how strongly the relationship has grown between all of us. I am really glad it did."

"So am I, Mary. We love you." Mickey sat quietly and smiled.

Mary continued, "You all accepted me right away. It means the world to me that my siblings never once called me their half-sister. They always introduced me as their sister."

"I do know that Michael, upon first hearing the news about having a sibling, commented, 'I guess I am not the oldest child in the family,' and Margaret said, 'I am not the only girl in the family any-more.' But after the initial reaction, they loved you and took you in immediately."

Mickey entered the conversation now and told Mary in his soft raspy voice about the Bronx and our life. He ended it with, "It didn't matter to me about anything that happened to Peg back in Ireland. I wanted to make sure she was okay. We had a great life together."

"Yes, we have, Mick." I reached over and held his hand. I continued, "It was a great weekend when you first came out."

"Yeah, Mom. Unbelievable. I met so many people that week-end I came out for Margaret's fortieth. It was overwhelming but a great time.

"All my life since I found out I was adopted, I thought you could be alive. During my teenage years, I thought it was kind of cool to say I was not born in the United States and I was born in Ireland. My mother did everything right, but one day it hit me you may be

227

alive and I think that seed stayed planted in my head for quite a while. Then when I married and had children, I did not have answers to many family medical questions. I could only answer, 'I don't know.'

"The thought of finding you grew stronger after I had kids of my own. I thought, *What if she's alive? How is she doing? I wonder if she thinks about me. I would be worried if it was my kid.* I wanted to tell you that I was alright.

"The letter I found in the folder said you went into nursing. I figured you went to nursing school. I didn't realize they meant you were a nanny raising a family. Maybe they didn't either. I knew women had babies at a young age and were sent away in Ireland, so I was calculating in my head that you could have been sixteen or seventeen when you had me.

"When I filled out the paperwork to get married, it was the first time I ever saw my naturalization papers. Since I didn't have my birth certificate to get a marriage license, my dad gave me these papers, which actually had my kindergarten picture on it.

"My parents did not like it when I asked questions about the adoption. Dad was more forthcoming with answers than Mom. I only found out I was adopted when that girl on the block said something to me. My mom never said anything about it to me prior to that day. I was eight at the time. When we did talk about it later on, Mom gave me some information about how they went through Catholic Charities and how the organization had a thing over in Ireland and we received information from people. I followed up with, 'Well, what information?' She quickly shut me down and said, 'We got it. It's okay. You're here.' They really did not sit down and have a talk with me about it at all. When I inquired how I got here, my parents then showed me some pictures of me coming down off the plane and then my mom holding me, but these pictures are gone now. I think Tim discarded them by accident when he was cleaning out the house and moving.

"I do remember seeing some of the pictures and saying, 'I thought I was a baby when I came over. Mom is holding me and I looked older. She said, 'No, no. You were eighteen months old and were living at the convent.' She told the story that I was crying until they gave me to her. She said, 'You just quieted down. You knew I was your mom.'"

The conversation paused as we looked up at the bright shinning stars. There was a lot of information and emotions to digest. Mary spoke again, "I have always enjoyed our time together, Mom. I love that you are proud to introduce me to people as your daughter. When we go into Shortway's, you are not afraid to say, 'This is my daughter from Chicago.' Early on, some people were confused because they knew I was not Margaret, but as the story was told to more people they understood. You were like the Mayor of Shortway's just like at Nadia's. Are you the most popular person in town or what?"

"I love talking to you, Mary. Talking to you brings back many memories I haven't thought about in a long time. I am glad you feel comfortable opening up to me and sharing your story. The alcohol helps a little too," I chuckled.

Mary said, "Finding you also came with a lot of emotions and hard work. I lost my parents because they were older. After my mom died, I found you and I gained a mom again."

"I am so glad you found me. There was always a hole in my heart and now it is whole again."

"I feel blessed being able to have this time with you."

Mickey said, "We do too." He smiled again, said good night, and went inside.

Mary said, "I know it is tough to relive these stories, but I appreciate it, Mom."

"I have buried them deep down inside for so long. It is all in the past. I don't like to talk about it too much in front of Mickey. He was so kind to me and was my savior. I don't want to betray his love."

"Not at all, Mom. It is a beautiful story, how he found you and you two created such a great life together. I will always remember how Mickey greeted me at the airport with a bouquet of flowers. I fell in love with him immediately. He is a mountain of a man." We both took a sip of our drinks. The night air began to cool.

"I love you, Mom. Thank you for the gift of life, giving me a life, and coming into my life once again." It was getting late and we both went inside to go to sleep. We had to get up early for Mass in the morning.

That Sunday afternoon, Mary went into Mick's bedroom to say goodbye. Because of his weakness and inability to sleep at night, Mick took long naps in the afternoons. She said, "Mick, I am leaving now." He struggled to say goodbye, responded with an okay, and raised his hand a little to wave goodbye. Mary sat on the bed, gave him a big hug and said, "I'll see you soon." In response, he held Mary longer than he usually did. This time something was a little different. It was his way of saying goodbye. That summer was the last time Mary saw Mick.

Chapter 37

Dear Sister

December 2014

Dear Maggie,

I wanted to write you a letter this special season. How very blessed I am to have found you. Since I was a little girl I dreamed for a sister, and my dreams came true when I met you! Sounds corny, but it's true. If I could have sent God my perfect description, it would be you! I think about what must have gone through your mind when mom told you that you had a sister and you had to wait twenty more years. I've never met someone so gentle and loving of heart. I am still in awe of how there was no hesitation on your part to share your life with me. Remember what you said when I asked if it bothered you when Pat introduced me as his sister?? I will always remember. You said, "It's music to my ears!" I was stunned. I love you for that.

I know this is a rough time with your dad. I realize he is your heart. I pray for him every day and for you. I wish I could be there to hold you when you're frightened and laugh with you when life is good. You have been such a support in our family. Thank God you are all together and there for each other. I miss you so much and am so sad I can't come this Christmas. Always know I love you and will be there if you need me. Thank you for sharing mom, my brothers, your children and giving me a family I cherish and thank God for every day. May your Christmas be joyful and full of family, laughter, and love.

To make up for not being around during the "big" sis advice years, I wish you this:

1. To continue to love unconditionally.
2. Don't let anyone bring down your spirit!
3. Continue being the compass for your students.
4. Know your relationship with mom is headed for some rough patches of frustration and anger, but you will be fine and we will love her together and that will give her strength to weather any storms ahead.
5. Know you are loved always.
6. Any decisions made in the past are in the past and were right for that moment in your life.
7. It's not about the breaths you take, it's about the moments that take your breath away!
8. I love you!

I love you and am
so very proud of you
Mags

Chapter 38

That December Chill

Tragedy did not only affect the old in our family. Unfortunately, it hit the young too. In June 2014, our 19-year-old grandson, Patrick, Pat and Beth Ann's middle child, suffered an unfortunate head injury playing softball with friends. Patrick was pitching to a teammate in preparation for an upcoming charity softball game that raised money for The Matthew Larson Foundation for Pediatric Brain Tumors. "IronMatt" was a local boy who passed away from this terrible disease at age seven. Nick, brother of IronMatt, was the batter and a good friend of Patrick. Nick hit a hard line drive back to the mound. Patrick, being a college athlete with quick reflexes, dodged the direct hit, but the softball, which is a misnomer and not soft at all, struck Patrick on the left side of the head. He was shook up but able to walk off the field and go to Nick's house. After returning home, Patrick's parents decided to take him to Valley Hospital to get checked out after complaints of a headache. Shortly after midnight when the CAT scan and other test results came in, Patrick was immediately rushed to New York-Presbyterian Hospital for surgery.

The doctor told Patrick's parents, Pat and Beth Ann, that only twenty percent of people who sustained traumatic brain injuries similar to Patrick's survived and only two percent fully recovered. The next few hours and days would determine his fate. The family was being tested but, as we usually do, banned together to support Patrick.

A day or two after Patrick was admitted, Carol, a family friend, visited the hospital and shared with Beth Ann an encounter she recently had with a spiritual medium. The medium said that Patrick had to go to Nick's house after being struck by the softball before going home because he was guided there by IronMatt to make a spiritual connection between the two of them. Nick's mother was an Emergency Medical Technician and told Patrick to go to the hospital right away. Pat and Beth Ann rushed Patrick to Valley Hospital to get checked out.

The doctor at Valley was also affiliated with New York-Presbyterian, and after doing initial tests informed Pat and Beth Ann that Patrick's best chance of survival would be in the city. In the early hours of the morning, an ambulance sped down Route 17 to Route 4 to transport Patrick to New York, where he was immediately placed in the Intensive Care Unit (ICU).

The neurosurgeon who saw Patrick at Valley and later at New York-Presbyterian was the same doctor who treated IronMatt. Coincidentally, or maybe not, Patrick was also admitted to the same hospital room as IronMatt. The medium further informed Carol that IronMatt said all would be okay with Patrick and that he was in good hands. IronMatt was a Guardian Angel for Patrick.

Luck, faith, and love all came together to save Patrick as he slowly showed signs of improvement in the ICU of the hospital. But he was not out of the woods yet, and his recovery was still unpredictable. Wanting to do something to show their support for the O'Hagan family, a Wyckoff friend set up a prayer vigil at St. Elizabeth Church.

We did not know how many would show for the prayer vigil. We were prepared for thirty family members or the three hundred community members who actually came out that evening. Walking into the church, the energy from all present was felt. After the priest led us in prayers and said a few words, Pat spoke to the congregation. He first stated that he and his family felt no ill will towards Nick who hit the softball that struck Patrick. It was an accident, and Pat asked us to pray for Nick and his family. Next, he thanked the community and asked for everyone's love, prayers, and support. He spoke from the heart and comforted us all. He was definitely inspired by the Holy Spirit that evening.

After the vigil ended, Pat received a phone call from Beth Ann, who was still at the hospital at Patrick's bedside. We were gathered around the baptismal font in the middle of the church, and she shared the good news that the doctor gave the okay for Patrick to be moved from the ICU to a regular hospital room. This decision was made in New York while we were all praying in New Jersey.

After two weeks, Patrick was released from the hospital. He was still weak and slept a lot. To ease the swelling from the injury, the doctor had to remove part of Patrick's skull to save his life. He needed two more surgeries to insert a titanium plate in his head and reconstruct his skull, but each day he was home he became stronger.

On one of Patrick's first days home from the hospital, Mickey and I drove over to visit Patrick. Many family members were gathered in the family room when we arrived. Mick struggled to get out of the car and get up the three stairs into Pat and Beth Ann's house, but his sons helped him. As soon as Mick entered the house and saw Patrick, however, it was as if a switch flipped and it was game time. Mick walked tall and strong as he approached Patrick.

Mick sat down on the edge of the couch where Patrick was lying on his right side. Mickey, his eyes red and teary, held Patrick's hand firmly. Mickey's hands were dry, calloused, and strong. When he held you in his grip there was no escape. With a dry, scratchy, and soft voice, he gave Patrick words of encouragement and love. Their conversation was soft-spoken and could not be heard by too many around them, but from across the room everyone could see and feel the love and emotion being shared in this moment.

In a soft weak voice, Patrick told his grandfather, "I thought I was going to die in the hospital bed at the age of nineteen. But it was the thought of you living with cottonmouth for sixteen years that allowed me to make this unbearable side effect bearable. How could I complain about my injury and situation when you have been battling with your weakened body all these years? I knew I had to suck it up and keep fighting."

While in the hospital, the doctors prescribed Patrick medication to reduce the swelling in the brain that had the side effect of giving him the sensation of severe thirst. While the medication was saving his life, it also made him extremely irritable and thirsty. Similarly, as a result of Mick's salivary glands being destroyed due to the radiation treatments, Mick always had a dry mouth. Patrick began to understand how his grandfather truly felt. However, unlike Mickey's situation, Patrick knew his was only temporary. Patrick continued to tell his grandfather on that couch, "You are a role model and a motivation for me to get better."

Mick was a spiritual man but also one of practicality. He put his faith in God; however, he also knew that he had to do *his* part. He shared the secret to his success of survival with his grandson. Still holding his hand and moving very close to his face, Mick told Patrick, "I love you very much. The secret to surviving is to get your mind on a certain level that you never thought possible. The battle is not physical but mental, and with the right attitude anything is attainable."

Patrick said, "Grandpa, you are the epitome of a fighter. You are the reason that I am here today. The example you set every day of living on a feeding tube and not having any saliva to swallow gave me the confidence that I could beat this injury. You saved my life. Thank you. I love you." Mick and Patrick embraced each other for a long while and didn't say anything else.

Over the next three years, Patrick and I grew even closer. Because of his seizures and recovery, he could not drive and did not return to college for the first year. Since I was retired and had time on my hands, I became Patrick's personal chauffeur and confidant. I went over to the house every day and talked to Patrick.

Our days typically started with Patrick cooking me eggs and toast and making me a cup of coffee. He enjoyed accomplishing simple tasks and taking care of me – the irony. We spent hours together talking about what happened to him. Patrick reaffirmed how lucky he was to be alive, and I told him how proud Mickey and I were of him. We repeated ourselves often, but it was good to talk about the ordeal for Patrick to process it all. He asked many questions about Mick, and I shared stories about the old days of his father's and siblings' upbringing.

On December 29, 2014, Patrick experienced a terrible grand mal seizure, the first since his accident, so the worry was overwhelming for all. He recovered and was not harmed. The following day, our worry continued to grow, but now it was for Mickey who was not looking well. For sixteen years he fought his personal battle, but by this time Mickey had enough.

I called Margaret to let her know Daddy had taken a nasty spill and he was unable to get himself back up. She rushed over to our home and sat on our bed just as she did sixteen years before to tell Mick she was expecting. Both of their hands had aged, but the tender hold was just the same. She was crying. "Daddy," she whispered, "I'll never tell you not to fight, but you are suffering, and you fought too hard to suffer." In a soft, raspy voice he said back to her, "Margaret, I'm just sick and tired of being sick and tired." She wiped away her own tears along with her daddy's and said the words I had been afraid to actually believe, "We will all be okay." His little girl gave him permission to go.

I had to trust my daughter that we would, after all, be okay. It was difficult to come to terms with the fact we were losing our Mickey. I fell asleep next to my husband, and worry began to fill my heart. *Was this it? Were we really losing our tough guy? Is this the end?* These dreary thoughts lulled me to sleep.

That night, I woke up around 2:00 A.M. with a tight hold on Mickey's arm. That end-of-December chill filled our home and he was cold, so I groggily got out of bed to get him a heavier blanket. When I returned to the room, I stood in the doorway and stared at Mickey. The blanket fell at my feet. Our tough guy, the love of my life, was gone and his big crazy ocean blue eyes could not reassure me all would be okay ever again.

Chapter 39

Wonderful Life

On January 1, 2014, the chill that had been in our home now filled the air, and yet the line for the wake wrapped around the inside of the funeral parlor and continued outside through the parking lot. There must have been close to one thousand people paying their respects. That is one way you can tell the influence you have made on the world. It reminded me of the movie *It's a Wonderful Life*. Mickey and I watched that movie many times.

The funeral was held at St. Anthony Church, and the pews were filled. As we processed up the aisle behind the coffin, I dipped my hand into the baptismal font to bless myself. Being so nervous and a little oblivious to my surroundings at the time, I accidently knocked over the aspergillum and aspersorium, the silver ball on a stick and bucket used to sprinkle holy water on congregants during special masses. The sound of metal hitting the terrazzo floor rattled the people gathered and broke the ice of the sadness of the moment.

During the homily, the priest gave me credit for taking care of Mickey for sixteen years while he was ill. He said I should have received an honorary degree in nursing for all that I did. While that was nice of him to say, I didn't see it that way. I was proud to be able to take care of the man who took care of me all the years we were together. The man I loved in sickness and in health. The man who saved me when I came to America.

To send Mickey off properly, we held a good Irish repast that lasted twelve hours. Fittingly, it was held at an Elks Club, the organization he belonged to all of his years while living in New Jersey, and all were invited to attend. Close to three hundred people came for food and drinks, and to share memories. After people paid their respects and most of the food was gone, the gathering dwindled down to mostly immediate family and friends. The party moved into the small dark barroom of the Club. There was a jukebox in the corner that played songs all afternoon and night as long as it was fed with quarters, and the beer kept flowing as long as the bartender was given dollars. That night, there was dancing, singing, laughter, and tears. The evening ended with a minor scuffle at the bar with a local patron who made a few inappropriate comments to us. That was a big mistake on his part. It was a great way to send Mickey off. I knew he was smiling down upon us from heaven above.

Five days prior to his death, Mickey garnered enough strength to come down to the basement on Christmas Eve. In the middle of the room, surrounded by the family, he bent down on one knee and proposed to me again. It was the best Christmas present I ever received.

Christmas changed for me over the years. In Ireland, it was a special day to go to church and maybe have a little something extra at the supper table. It wasn't until I met Mickey and we began a family that the holiday started to change in its meaning. However, Christmas was also a time I became a little melancholic and thought of Mary. After we moved to Hawthorne, we spent every Christmas Eve as a family in the basement. It was always a special night. Although Mary came into the picture in the final years before Mickey's passing, the sadness I felt at Christmas did not totally dissipate. The sadness I felt that Mary was not in my life was replaced by the sadness that Mick was losing his strength and not participating in the holiday as he always had. Now, four days after his death, a dozen police officers led the procession from the church, past Ninth Ave., to the cemetery.

Even after Mickey's passing, he was still taking care of me from the grave. Without my knowledge, he paid all of our bills six months in advance. Again, I could see him smiling at me from above. Also, since we had not been going out to the bars for dinner and drinks these past sixteen years, we were able to accumulate a little nest egg that helped me in retirement. However, I now had to lay out my daily pills in the weekly pill box for myself. That used to be Mickey's job.

I continued to see Patrick every day and he cooked me my breakfast. Our conversations still revolved around his injury and recovery, but now they included more stories of Mickey. It was as though our conversations were our own little bereavement group – I was grieving the loss of Mickey, and Patrick was grieving the loss of his youth. Because of the injury, Patrick lost out on what many nineteen-year-olds were supposed to experience and enjoy. It was a year before he could attend college again, but after a semester of returning to Cortland University he realized it was just too much. He enrolled as a commuter student at a local school, Ramapo College. He also had to come to grips with the fact that he would never finish his college football career.

In one of our conversations, Patrick shared with me, "Mum-Mum, I have been thinking a lot about my injury and what it means. I know I don't have all the answers, but watching you and Grandpa all these years has taught me what is important in life. You were always there for others whenever they needed something. You and Grandpa never said no or blew people off. Maybe life is about struggle and adversity. It's not about doing things for yourself but for people you love around you. I wonder what God has planned for me."

"Patrick, in the final months before Mickey passed, he shared with me, 'Maybe my suffering for sixteen years was to set an example for the grandchildren. Maybe my suffering did save Patrick's life. Why do things happen? If you never had gotten pregnant, then you would not have come to America, and we would not have had the life we do. We would not have had the beautiful grandchildren that we have.'"

I grabbed Patrick's hand, "God has wonderful plans for you. It will all be revealed to you in God's time."

"I looked up to him so much," Patrick said.

"He knew and loved you so."

"I loved him too."

"Besides the birth of my children and grandchildren, three miracles have occurred in my life. The first was my marriage to Mickey, the second was reuniting with Mary, and the third was your recovery to full health. God has been very good to me."

I continued to drive Patrick to help him with his errands, drop him off at the YMCA for workouts, and drive him to Ramapo for classes. Patrick got a kick out of the Irish music I played in the car. Our favorite song was "The Foggy Dew." We kept each other company when times were tough.

In the years since Mickey's passing, Mary still came to visit and we still talked on the phone. She said I opened up to her even more now. Previously, I was holding some things back, not wanting to hurt or betray Mickey. That is why I did not want to tell this story until after he passed. Mary was the same way. She did not begin to look for me until after her parents passed. She, too, did not want to betray her loved ones.

It has been said O'Hagans repeat themselves regarding the telling of their stories. This may be true, but some stories are worth retelling. When Mickey was in the hospital or at home recovering, these moments slowed down time and allowed the family to gather more often than the usual of every few weeks to share their favorite stories. The grandchildren grew older and began to show interest in the stories of their parents. Ninth Ave. was and continued to be the bedrock of our family foundation. These stories kept our loved ones with us after they departed from this world.

Mary told me she wanted to see me as much as she possibly could. She came out sometimes with her family and sometimes by herself. I always looked forward to her visits. We frequented Nadia's and Shortway's, and at night sat on the back deck sharing stories. Looking back, I would not have had the beautiful life I have lived had it not been for Mary. Mary was the rock thrown into the water that caused many ripples across the pond. I would not have come to America and had the family that I have if it wasn't for her. I love my Mickey, family, and Mary. When you think about it, it was a wonderful life.

Afterword

Dearest Mom,

I am writing you to let you know how truly proud I am to call you my mother. Over these past ten years of our miracle I have learned so many ways to love and be loved. When the decision to find you began forming in my mind, I didn't know what would happen. Many questions came into my head...Will she want to see me? Will she be worried about why I am looking for her? Does she know that she gave me a perfect life and what she did was heroic and unselfish? Well mom, I want to thank you for loving me so much that letting me go must have been the hardest thing you've ever had to do. I want to thank you for welcoming me back into your life and changing my life forever. You have given me more than I could ever have imagined when I began this journey.

Now we have a book being written about us. What do you think about that? Our story is one of innocence lost and love found. Of a young girl who found herself when she put her baby first. You are my hero and you must always know the decision you made as a young girl may have been a hard one, but it was the right one. You found a family that loved me and gave me a life I could only have dreamed of...And YOU did that for me. Thank you!

What lies ahead of us can only be better each day. Though we are separated by miles, we will never be separated by the heart. How lucky I am to have had one beautiful woman raise me and then been sent another selfless woman to love me through my years to come. Here's to us, and a life spent in celebration of that young girl so many years ago who said, "I want a better life for my child," because I am here to tell you Margaret Holland O'Hagan, my life is better than you ever could have imagined. I love you with all that I am and all that I will ever be. THANK YOU!

Love,

Mary

Acknowledgments

My love for Mary never wavered. Even though she was absent from much of my life, she was with me and I with her for the years we were separated. I am so glad we were able to reconnect and share the stories from our lost time together and make new ones in the years after our reunion.

A special thank you to Louisa Vilardi for her guidance, support, and help with making this story come to fruition. Being my first written work, it was a difficult task, but her reassurance and constant support helped bring this book to reality.

The cover of this memoir came to life through the help of Angela Ross. Angela has been a great friend to Margaret and Tom for many years and is a very talented artist.

Thank you to my children, Mary, Michael, Jimmy, Pat, and Margaret; the Outlaws, Tom, Robyn, Judy, Beth Ann, and Tom; and grandchildren, Jamie, Erin, Carly, Juliann, Patrick, Erica, Mike, Joe, Sean, Hagan, Shea, Meghan, and Alex for their understanding and love my whole life. Our love for each other is palpable and has supported us through the years.

Thank you to John and Sandy O'Hagan for sharing their stories and reminding me of some of the finer details of our times together. They have been loving family members and two people Mick and I could rely on throughout our life.

I appreciate my English nephews, Mark and Paul, for helping fill in the details of my youth. They heard many stories from their father, Jim, and could recite them as if they were their own.

Mary would like to extend the greatest appreciation for all the love and support from the Boler, Timmons, and Doran families. She especially wants to acknowledge Sister Mary McManus of Cork for all her assistance in making this miracle come true.

Favorite Expressions

Over the years, many sayings and expressions have come out of my mouth, and I don't know where they come from sometimes. Don't ask me what they all mean because I don't really know. I picked them up throughout life and some just stayed with me since my youth. My children and grandchildren get a kick out of them, so I listed a number of them here for your pleasure.

At least we're on the right side of the grave.

Black as soot.

Brush your teeth, your breath is red rotten.

Don't read too much.
(A warning to women to not drive themselves crazy with all the information available when pregnant.)

Excuse the pig, the bacon's Irish.

Feck 'em and feed 'em beans.

Feck off.

For fucks sake.

Fresh air knocks 'em out.

Here's your hat, what's your hurry.

I love you a bushel and a peck.
(Lyrics from the Broadway musical "Guys and Dolls" said to the grandchildren.)

If everyone put their troubles in the street, you would grab yours and run like hell.

I'll give you a tip, don't piss into the wind.

It's good to be seen.
(In response to someone saying, "Good to see you.")

It's half past pissing time, time to piss again.

Jesus, Mary, Joseph, and all the saints preserve us.

Kiss my ass.
(Pog mo thoin.)

Kiss my royal Irish ass.

Let them sleep. They grow when they're sleeping.
(In reference to children napping.)

Look at you, your eyes are blue, you look like a monkey, in the zoo.

Put Vaseline on it.
(Cure for all cuts, scrapes, and broken bones.)

Someone's pregnant.
(In reference when someone picked up two forks or knives at the same time at a meal.)

Take off your sock and piss in your shoe.
(Usually said after the grandchildren expressed how they were bored.)

The days are long but the years fly by.

Use bleach to clean it.
(Bleach was used to disinfect all surfaces, and wash white and colored clothes. Tide laundry detergent was also thrown in the bathtub to help clean the kids.)

We were poor but who the feck knew.

You will eat a pound of dirt before you die.

Appendix

| Cláruimhir Registration Number | 5346097 | Breith a Chláraíodh i gCeantar Birth Registered in the district of | Roscrea No. 1 |
| i limistéar an Phríomh-Chláraitheora in the Superintendent Registrar's District of | Roscrea | i gContae in the County of | Co. Tipperary |

Uimh.	Dáta Breithe Date of Birth	Ainm	Gnéas	Ainm, Sloinne agus Ionad Chónaithe an Athar	Ainm agus Sloinne na Máthar agus|a sloinne roimh phósadh dí	Céim nó Gairm Bheatha an Athar	Siniú, Cáilíocht agus Ionad Chónaithe an Fhaisnéiseora	An Dáta a Chláraíodh	Siniú an Chláraitheora	Ainm tugac ch Breit
No.	Ionad Breithe Place of Birth	Name	Sex	Name and Surname and Dwelling-Place of Father	Name and Surname and Maiden name of Mother	Rank or Profession of Father	Signature, Qualification and Residence of Informant	When Registered	Signature of Registrar	B# Nam Regi Birt
10	1985 April Twenty Fourth Roscrea	Mary	F	-	Peggy Holland formerly	-	Helen Finnegan Mary ... Dean Ross Abbey Roscrea	Mary ... 19 85	... ... CLÁ (Regi

Mary Margaret Holland's Birth Certificate.

253

CERTIFICATE OF BAPTISM

PARISH OF Roscrea   DIOCESE OF Killaloe

I HEREBY CERTIFY that Mary Holland

was born on the 24th day of April 19.5.5 and was
Baptised according to the Rite of the Catholic Church on the 29th day of
April 19.5.5 in the Church of St. Michael
by the Rev. Gerard J. Fitzpatrick

Sponsor Kathleen Masterson

Signed: Rev. Patrick Whelan   -P.P./Curate

Date 25th January 1957

Mary's Certificate of Baptism in Ireland.

254

1957

Jan 1st. Harry called Ireland
talked to Sister Hildegarde
They are a little disappointed
Our baby won't be here
until after the 21st.
11 Harry sent a letter to Ireland
14 Pan American called Mary
will be arriving Jan 26th, 7:20 am.
23 Miss Condie from P.A.A called
We have refund 112.79
(cancele girls)
25 La Verne gave me a shower
26 Picked up our daughter at
O'Hara airport 12:25 pm. Took Peggy
home. Fed her + put her to bed
We were surprised to hear her
talk. (airplane Due at 7:20)
Feb. 8. A Schroeddt gave a shower
for Peggy.
April 8 Swanson Studio took
Peggy pictures. 12 proof
April 24 + Birthday Party.
May 23. Bob confirmation
June 3 - Jack died
June 7 Vacation in Gatlinburg

Dorothy Timmon's journal notes.

255

10th. December 1956.

My dear Friends,

We see from your letter just received that it was posted on the 5th. that is a long time but I suppose the delay is sue to the Christmas rush,

You will be glad to know that we have forwarded a picture of Mary Holland to Revd. Fr. Brogan of Catholic Charitie for your inspection, this is our usual procedure. The picture has only gone in the last evenings post and will arraive about the sam time as this letter as there is only one collection on Sunday. If you call Father he will let you see the picture. Mary is a lit Pet and you should be very happy with her and she with you.

As time is getting along so quickly we cannot now hope to have Mary with you for Christmas but pleas God you will have her early in the New Year, her chances for a passport before Christmas would be only 100 - 1. Of coure if you have got started on your papers it may work but dont be disappointed.

We have two children going into Chiaago on the 18th., they are not staying there, just landing and being met my adopting Parents from another State.

P.A.A. will contact you and collect the fare when we have everthing ready here. You expenses to ths Institution for the preapration of the child will be $145.00. which will not be paid until you are sure you are all through.

Please remember us all in your prayers and we will pray for you.

Should it happen that we do not hear from you between this and Christmas we wish you every Grace and Bless and we wish to thank you for the money for postage, this we think speaks well of your thoughfulness and makes us feel more happy about little Mary's future. God and Our Lady bless and keep you

Sincerely in the Sacred Hearts.

SR. M. Hildegarde

Letter to Harry and Dorothy Timmons from
Sr. Hildegarde prior to Mary's adoption.
256

January 11, 1957

Sister Hildegard
Sean Ross Abbey
Roscrea
County Tipperary

Dear Sister:

The time is growing near as to when we can expect little Mary to
be with us and she will probably be a little surprised to find us
with two feet of snow and temperatures below zero. However, we
live on top of a hill and I am sure she will enjoy sleding opportunities that awaits her.

I was very glad New Years Day that I had an opportunity to talk
to you via overseas phone. The few minutes of conversation put
my wife's and my mind at ease, as we did not know exactly when
we could expect her.

She seems to have taken over the house already without even being
here, with the erection of her bed and items she has received for
Christmas from her future grandparents, uncles and aunts. We
were rather disappointed, which is understandable, when the 100
to 1 chance did not pay for us so that she could be here for
Christmas, but as I write this I realize that it is only a matter
of a week or so and she will be in our family.

We pre-paid her flight on the Pan American before Christmas upon
instructions to do so from the Pan American. We just wanted to
make sure that we would not be the cause of any delay.

We were very much taken with the picture that you sent us of her
and my wife claims she favors me, but I can't see it yet.

We hope that all goes well and the final clearances are made in
Dublin so that we may expect her around the time you told me on
New Years Day.

Hoping that our next communication will be one telling us when
to expect her. I remain

                          Very sincerely yours,

                          Harry M. Timmons Jr.
                          Route #13 Emerson Avenue
                          Glen Ellyn, Illinois

Letter from Harry Timmons to Sr. Hildegarde
about Mary's upcoming adoption.

February 18, 1957

Sister Hildegard
Roscrea Abbey
Roscrea County Tipperary

Dear Sister:

Mary has been with us now for over three weeks, and I cannot tell you how pleased we are with her. She is everything we expected and more. My son and her have hit it off very well, although now he finds it a little more difficult to do his homework, with her at his elbow.

In Church she behaves like a perfect little lady, although in our Church we have one room set aside, to the side of the altar, which is sound proof and referred to as the "cry room". It gives us a great deal of pleasure the way she behaves, while in church, compared to the other children her age. She displays a considerable amount of initiative and has made herself quite at home. She is quite devoted to my wife.

We had her to our family doctor, for she had a touch of diarrhea, and our doctor said she was in excellent health, but he would be interested in knowing her medical history, particularly what type of inoculations she had already, other than those specified on her papers.

My wife and son and I wish to express our heart filled thanks to you for selecting this wonderful child for us. We have renamed her Margaret Mary and call her Peggy.

Enclosed you will find a New York draft to cover the expenses.

Sincerely yours,

Harry M. Timmons Jr.
Emerson Ave. Route #13
Glen Ellyn, Illinois

HMT:jt

Letter to Sr. Hildegarde from
Harry Timmons after Mary's adoption.
258

1st. March 1957.

My very dear Friends,

Your letter was like a ray of sunshine or
a word from Heaven. We were very fond of little Peggy and miss her
a lot in spite of all the others we have but she was one on her
own in her sweet gentle way. Now it has taken my breath away
that you have re-named her - Margaret Mary and are calling her
Peggy, this is what her mother was known as and she was one of the
most beautiful, gentle, refined girls I have put through my hands,
she has gone on for Nursing and is doing well but she is one of
the people who will always remember the past and be sorry about it

Now about Mary or Peggy as you call her. She
had no Shots except those named on her paper, Diphtheria and
Whooping Cough combined and she was as you know Vaccinated. We
dont do the B.C.G. except there is a history of T.B. and we have
not started Polio shots in this Country as we had only one out-
break in my life-time.

What may be giving Peggy the Diarrhea could be
fruit, we found she was not able for a lot of Oranges, this brings
on loose stools for many of them. When she is a little older she
probably will be able for all such things. Over six months ago
she had a prolapse on about four occasions, our Doctor prescribed more heat and less running about for a week or two, it completely cleared so I dont think you have great reason to worry
about her. She never had a serious sickness apart from that.

We got the Cheque for which we are more than
grateful.

Again my greatful thanks for the lovely letter
and for your kindness to Peggy. God and His Holy Mother bless
and protect you and yours. Pray for me.

Sincerely in the Sacred Hearts.

Sr. M. Hildegarde

Letter to Harry and Dorothy Timmons
from Sr. Hildegarde after Mary's adoption.

259

My Dearest Peggie

I love you Mrs. Peggie so very much, I just can't wait until I'm home to be with you, I need you so very much, I wish I could could tell you how much I love you & need you. I don't know what I'd do without you. I'm so bugged up & fouled up right now I don't know what to do with myself. Your birthday is Wednesday & then I don't even have money to send you a card. I feel real bugged up about it. I love you Peggie so very much I wish so much I could be with you but it won't be long now when we will be together for the rest of our lives, I'm going to love you so much when I get home. I'm not going to let you out of my arms for at least a week & you better not give me a hard time, my shaving isn't much.

Well Lou John was down this weekend & me had a few beer together. (He paid for them). It will probably be the last time I'll see him until he comes home if we don't stop on our way home & see him for a couple of hours.

Well Lou things are pretty much the same down here, I had a pretty busy day today. It was pretty funny. A General came around today to look

Mick's letter to me while in the Army.

Mick's daily log of his weight and journal of what happened.

261

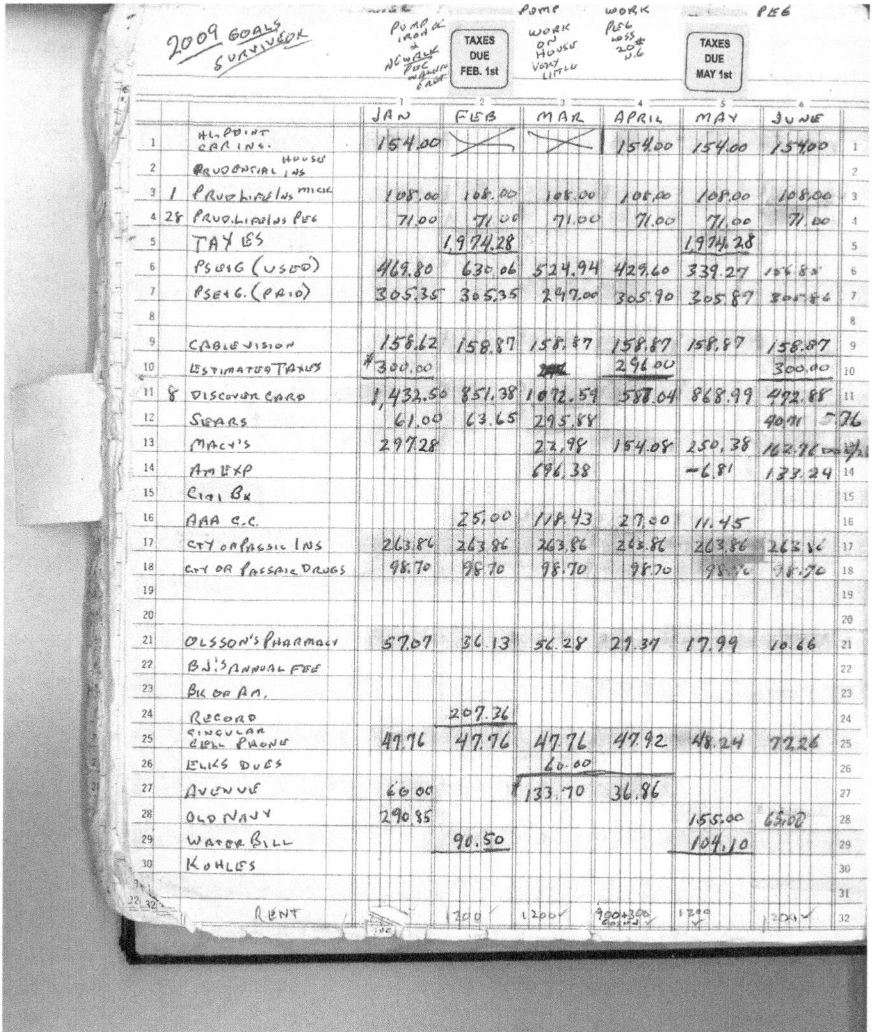

Handwritten ledger (2009 Goals / Survivor). Top margin notes include "PUMP & IRON @ NEWARK...", "POME WORK ON HOUSE VERY LITTLE", "WORK PEG LESS 20% U.G", "PEG", "TAXES DUE FEB. 1st", "TAXES DUE MAY 1st".

#		Item	JAN	FEB	MAR	APRIL	MAY	JUNE
1		HI-POINT CAR INS.	154.00			154.00	154.00	154.00
2		PRUDENTIAL INS HOUSE						
3	1	PRUD.LIFE INS MICK	108.00	108.00	108.00	108.00	108.00	108.00
4	28	PRUD.LIFE INS PEG	71.00	71.00	71.00	71.00	71.00	71.00
5		TAXES		1,974.28			1,974.28	
6		PSE&G (USED)	469.80	630.06	524.94	429.60	339.27	186.83
7		PSE&G (PAID)	305.35	305.35	247.00	305.90	305.87	305.86
8								
9		CABLE VISION	158.62	158.87	158.87	158.87	158.87	158.87
10		ESTIMATED TAXES	300.00			296.00		300.00
11	8	DISCOVER CARD	1,432.50	851.38	1072.54	587.04	868.99	472.88
12		SEARS	61.00	63.65	295.88		40.91	5.76
13		MACY'S	297.28		22.98	154.08	250.38	162.96
14		AM EXP			696.38		-6.81	133.24
15		CITI BK						
16		AAA C.C.		25.00	118.43	27.00	11.45	
17		CTY OR PASSIC INS	263.86	263.86	263.86	263.86	263.86	263.86
18		CITY OR PASSAIC DRUGS	98.70	98.70	98.70	98.70	98.70	98.70
19								
20								
21		OLSSON'S PHARMACY	57.07	36.13	56.28	29.34	17.99	10.66
22		BJ'S ANNUAL FEE						
23		BK OF AM.						
24		RECORD			207.36			
25		SINGULAR CELL PHONE	47.76	47.76	47.76	47.92	48.24	72.26
26		ELKS DUES			60.00			
27		AVENUE	60.00		133.70	36.86		
28		OLD NAVY	290.85				155.00	65.00
29		WATER BILL		90.50			104.10	
30		KOHLES						
31								
32		RENT		200	1200	900+300	1200	200

Mick's log of monthly bills and annual goals.

262

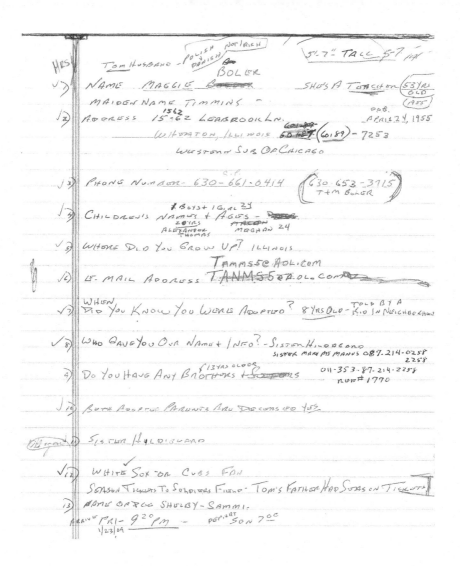

Mick's questions and notes during his first conversation with Mary.

Dear Peg (mom),

Well, what a ride we've been on! I am sitting here the night before I am to leave. So many thoughts are whirling in my head. So many questions to ask. But as I sit here I think about the miracle that has been handed to us. What are the chances that we would find each other? How very hard that must have been to give up your child. No one including me could ever know all the heartache. But so many factors invade our lives that steel our courses. Your selfless act of love gave me a life so filled with love and security. I owe you my life. I know after having my own children that what you did to give me a better life was the best gift a mother could give her child. I was blessed with a mom who committed her life to raising me with a firm foundation rooted in family. I wanted for nothing and my dad always believed we were related some how.

Mary's letter to Peg (Mom) written
the night before seeing her for the first time.

December 25, 2010

Dear Family,

I don't know who was elected to read this but here goes. A very Merry Christmas to all of you and I can't wait to see you Wednesday. Enclosed you will find some dorky gifts from me to you! I hope you like them and think of us when you use them and say, "Wow is she a dork!" On a more serious note, whatever you may think about giving me... take it back!! You have already given me a gift to last my whole life. When we found each other my life was complete. Everyday I am in awe of how you arms opened and swooped me into your life. I know the credit for your unconditional

Mary's first Christmas Eve letter to the family.
Because of their length, the annual letters
have been nicknamed the "Magna Carta."

265

Notes

The events of this memoir are portrayed to the best of our memories. While all the stories in this book are true, some names and identifying details have been altered or omitted to protect the privacy of the people involved.

The letters in this book were kept true to their original form. The font and type were kept as close to the original as possible. All misspellings in the letters and documents were not corrected so as to keep to the authenticity of the originals.

Several articles and websites were helpful in filling in the background of this story and the ordeals of women who went through similar circumstances. Although I was not aware of how widespread the problem was or of all the politics involved, it did help to learn I was not alone in my situation. Also, while I referred to a nurse who helped me at the abbey with my delivery, research indicates that it was most likely a midwife.

Adoption Rights Alliance. Retrieved 2019, from http://adoption.ie/my-front-page/our-work/ireland-us-adoptions/

Avoid the 'paddy wagon' this St. Patrick's Day. (2018, March 16). *National Law Enforcement Museum*. Retrieved from https://www.policeone.com/national-law-enforcement-museum/articles/avoid-the-paddy-wagon-this-st-patricks-day-snC4NkSsxiW18QOq/

Blakemore, E. (2019, July 21). How Ireland turned 'fallen women' into slaves. *History Channel*. Retrieved from https://www.history.com/news/magdalene-laundry-ireland-asylum-abuse

Bracken, A. (2014, June 29). Adoption, illegitimate children and the 'bogey of proselytism' in Catholic Ireland. *the Journal.ie*. Retrieved from https://www.thejournal.ie/readme/adoption-ireland-boarding-out-catholic-church-1534801-Jun2014/

Farrell, J. (2019, February 1). Spare a thought for Irish nuns who thought selling babies was merciful. *IrishCentral*. Retrieved from https://www.irishcentral.com/opinion/others/irish-nuns-catholic-selling-babies-homes-merciful

Laskow, S. (2017, March 16). The invisible unmarried mothers of Ireland. *Atlas Obscura*. Retrieved from https://www.atlasobscura.com/articles/ireland-tuam-mother-baby-homes-unmarried-graves

McGarry, P. (2019, April 19). Single mothers and their children paid price for 'innate deference' to Church. *The Irish Times*. Retrieved from https://www.irishtimes.com/news/social-affairs/religion-and-beliefs/single-mothers-and-their-children-paid-price-for-innate-deference-to-church-1.3865199

O'Reilly, R. (2019, May 21). Sean Ross Abbey - 1000 dead. *Raidió Teilifís Éireann*. Retrieved from https://www.rte.ie/news/investigations-unit/2019/0424/1045347-rte-investigates-sean-ross1000-dead/

O'Sullivan, C. (2014, July 21). A quarter of babies sent to US from Sean Ross Abbey. *Irish Examiner.* Retrieved from https://www.irishexaminer.com/ireland/a-quarter-of-babies-sent-to-ufrom-sean-ross-abbey-276105.html

Pioneer Total Abstinence Association. Retrieved 2019, from https://www.pioneerassociation.ie/

Redmond, P. (2020). Screaming rooms and banished babies: The sad history of where I was born. *Adoption News.* Retrieved from https://adoptionland.org/4163/screamingroomsandbanishedbabies/

Rivero, D. (2016, March 16). A complete history of the phrase 'paddy wagon,' the surviving Irish-American slur. *Splinter.* Retrieved from https://splinternews.com/a-complete-history-of-the-phrase-paddy-wagon-the-survi-1793855618

Sean Ross Abbey Images. Retrieved 2019, from https://www.google.com/search?q=images+of+Sean+ross+abbey&tbm=isch&ved=2ahUKEwj-3Lqzl83nAhVZZ98KH-WkcDBEQ2-cCegQIABAA&oq=images+of+sean+ross+abbey&gs_l=img.3..35i3912.4337.7264..7797...0.0..0.98.814.12......0....1..gws-wiz-img.Xa1uX5ukh_o&ei=V4xEXr7VENnO_QbpuLCIAQ&bih=636&biw=1379

Sean Ross Abbey Grounds Images. Retrieved 2019, from https://www.google.com/search?q=images+of+grounds+of+sean+ross+abbey&tbm=isch&ved=2ahUKEwiE1tDW9sznAhXuVd8KHWF0BpAQ2-cCegQIABAA&oq=images+of+grounds+of+sean+ross+abbey&gs_l=img.3...15693.16580..17151...0.0..0.67.367.6......0....1..gws-wiz-img.jZro0TQ0140&ei=BmpEXoS7KO6r_Qbh6JmACQ&bih=789&biw=1440

Made in the USA
Middletown, DE
23 July 2022

69931696R00156